Kimono
きもの
日本語 Level 2

Suzanne Burnham
with Yukiko Saegusa
and Michael Sedunary

Illustrated by Alex Jankovic

Consultants
Robyn Spence-Brown
Junko Glynn

Produced with the assistance of
The Japan Foundation

EMC Publishing, St. Paul, Minnesota

Edited by Curtis Watson
Designed and typeset by Josie Semmler
Illustrated by Alex Jankovic
Additional illustrations by Bill Farr
Crane character by Randy Glusac

© Sue Burnham and Yukiko Saegusa 1991

ISBN 0 8219 1039 6

All rights reserved. No part of this publication may be adapted, reproduced, stored in a retrieval system or transmitted in any form or by any means, electronic, mechanical, photocopying, recording, or otherwise without the permission from the publisher.

Published by EMC/Paradigm Publishing
875 Montreal Way
St. Paul, Minnesota 55102
800-328-1452
www.emcp.com
E-mail: educate@emcp.com

Printed in Singapore by Craft Print Pte Ltd
8 9 10 11 12 13 14 XXX 05 04 03 02 01 00

Contents・もくじ

Introduction vi
Acknowledgements viii

第一課　1
おみやげ です。どうぞ。

第二課　14
Maiku くん は どこ?

かたかな　27

第三課　31
へん じゃない ですよ。

第四課　47
チャッピー! こら!

第五課　62
ドーナツ は ぜんぜん
食べません。

第六課　76
ベビー シッター
は らく だなあ!

第七課　91
この いす の あし
は ありますか。

第八課　105
はし が つかえますか。

Appendix　118
漢字

単語
日本ー英語　120
英語ー日本語　123

第一課
おみやげです。
どうぞ。

Communicative tasks
Giving a self-introduction
Asking and saying what you do in your spare time
Asking and saying where activities happen
Giving and accepting compliments

Situations and vocabulary
After the summer holidays
Self-introductions
Leisure activities
Places to do things

Language points
じこしょうかい expressions
(ーねんせい、すんでいます)
で to show place
じょうず、とくい
...ちゃん

Cultural and linguistic background
Information on おみやげ, *pachinko* and borrowed words
Writing ひらがな

第二課
Maiku くん は どこ?

Communicative tasks
Inviting someone out
Accepting, declining and deferring invitations
Making a phone call
Asking and telling what people are doing now
Describing yourself and others

Situations and vocabulary
On the phone
Invitation expressions
Parts of the body
Adjectives

Language points
...ませんか as an invitation
Physical characteristics
い and な adjectives
ています

Cultural and linguistic background
A letter

カタカナ
Reading and writing カタカナ

第三課
へんじゃないですよ。

Communicative tasks
Finding out what is wrong with someone
Describing aches and pains
Describing things and people
Talking about nationalities and languages
Talking about the weather

Situations and vocabulary
Visiting someone who is sick
Expressions to describe illness
Countries, nationalities and languages
Weather terms

Language points
…がいたいんです。
いきます、きます、かえります
Negative of い and な adjectives
Nationalities (じん) and languages (ご)

Cultural and linguistic background
Trends in leisure activities in Japan
てんき
Learning the words — particular hints on learning vocabulary

第四課
チャッピー！こら！

Communicative tasks
Asking and telling where people and animals are
Asking for and giving information about family and pets
Stating what you don't do

Situations and vocabulary
At the vet
Items related to a student's room
Animals
Counters for people and animals

Language points
Place にいます／です
Spatial locations (うえ、した、うしろ、まえ)
Counters 人 and ひき
…と… as *and*

Cultural and linguistic background
Pop star culture

第五課
ドーナツはぜんぜんたべません。

Communicative tasks
Describing daily routine
Talking about clothing
Telling the time
Talking about how often you do things

Situations and vocabulary
At the triathlon
Clothing
Vocabulary relevant to daily routine

Language points
Time extended to ごふん、じゅっぷん
て form meaning *and*
Adverbs of time
Numbers 100 to 1000

Cultural and linguistic background
Activities during the school year in Japan
きせつ
Response expressions — how to be an active listener

第六課
ベビーシッター は らくだなあ！

Communicative tasks
Asking permission
Giving and refusing permission
Saying what you are not allowed to do
Talking about how much you like or dislike something

Situations and vocabulary
Baby-sitting
Colours
Household items

Language points
...てもいいですか。
...てはだめです。
すきじゃない、きらい

Cultural and linguistic background
High technology products
アンケート (Tokyo Disneyland)

第七課
この いす の あし は ありますか。

Communicative tasks
Asking and telling where things are
Shopping:
- asking what is available
- asking how much things cost
- deciding what to buy
- calculating the price

Situations and vocabulary
At the garage sale
Shops, and products, including fruit, vegetable and stationery items
Expressions for shopping

Language points
place にあります/です。
...はありますか。
ー や suffix for shops
Counters つ、さつ、本
...を ください。
Numbers 1000 to 10 000

Cultural and linguistic background
Japanese food
うた － かぞえましょう
Accentuate the positive －
focusing on positive reading skills

第八課
はし が つかえますか。

Communicative tasks
Asking and saying what you are able to do
Asking and telling what implements you use
Saying what language or script you use

Situations and vocabulary
In the classroom
Implements for writing and eating

Language points
...られます、...えます
できます
implement / tool で
language で
...へ to (a place)

Cultural and linguistic background
Travel in Hokkaido

もくじ

Introduction・はじめに

きもの 2 continues the lively, humorous approach to communicative language teaching adopted in the first level of the course. きもの 2 uses all of the communicative modes — listening, speaking, reading and writing — in a wide variety of activities.

The course emphasises language for use while taking a realistic approach to the need for carefully planned and clearly expressed grammatical explanations. Students are offered a great deal of communicative language supported by a systematic study of the structure of the language. In this way the course caters for a wide range of learning and teaching styles.

きもの 2 takes account of the increased language competence and the overall intellectual and social development of students of Japanese at this level.
In きもの 2 Japanese language is used more extensively, most noticeably in the cultural units, which use material reproduced from magazines and brochures. Furthermore, there is more flexibility in the structure of the book and a wider variety of language presentations and activities.

きもの 2 therefore represents the continuation of a proven method and format with refinements and developments designed to meet the changing needs of the maturing Japanese learner.

The Japanese script

In きもの Level 1 students learnt to read and write hiragana and a small number of kanji characters. Writing is seen as an integral part of the きもの course and in きもの Level 2 katakana, and more kanji, are presented.

Katakana is introduced in a section at the end of Unit 2 of the textbook. A more detailed introduction to katakana, with ample opportunity for practice, is provided in the workbook.

Sixteen kanji characters are also systematically introduced in the workbook. Many of these characters have been chosen for their frequency of use. It is suggested that the characters be taught prior to the commencement of each unit so as to maximise student recognition and use. The use of furigana has been limited to the vocabulary section of each unit.

The きもの 2 Textbook

The きもの 2 textbook comprises the elements outlined below.

まんが

The full-colour まんが at the beginning of each unit introduce students in a stimulating way to the language contained in the unit. The storylines combine humour and fantasy, giving incentive to become involved in the activities which follow.

As a teaching tool the まんが are particularly useful as a fund of knowledge to be exploited in both oral and written exercises. For these purposes the まんが need to be broken down into manageable sections and even a single cartoon frame could be used for pronunciation practice, role-playing, to illustrate a grammar point, or as a jump-off point for the creation of original dialogues.

いいましょう

The いいましょう exercises focus on particular language points, enabling intensive oral practice using the visual information provided.

In きもの 2 these exercises are designed for whole class, small group and pair work. Some いいましょう exercises provide for more than one 'correct' answer; this encourages students to consider their given responses.

The いいましょう exercises are also used at times to present vocabulary, and familiarity in advance with the new vocabulary will ensure that maximum benefit is gained from these exercises.

Students should find these exercises interesting and purposeful and a useful preparation for further oral activities.

Ideas for exploiting the いいましょう exercises are contained in the teacher's manual.

ともだちと

These pair-work exercises are the next stage towards unstructured conversation. Students are required to make a series of choices of words or phrases to construct a coherent dialogue. This process of deliberately selecting elements of dialogue gives students insights into the flexibility of discourse and into the way in which it is constructed.

いってみましょう

This oral activity is a most challenging and rewarding opportunity for students to put the language acquired in each unit to real communicative use. In this phase the task is relatively unstructured and students are expected to produce appropriate language.

In きもの 2 extensive use has been made of survey sheets, profiles and original materials in an effort to make these activities as interesting and as real and purposeful as possible.

Teachers play an important role in ensuring the success of these activities, by providing adequate preparation and by supporting and encouraging students in some quite challenging situations.

日本語ノート
This section aims to provide a simple, clear explanation of the language covered in each unit. Its role is to systematise certain aspects of grammar in a straightforward manner building on what students already know.

がんばれ
These sections are included in Units 1, 3, 5 and 7. The articles are intended to provide students with strategies for 'learning how to learn' and for coping in real language situations.

The articles are intended for discussion, a starting point for the sharing of learning hints and for reference. They should be dealt with in an order that best suits individual classes.

たんご
As students become exposed to more and more language the task of organizing the acquisition of vocabulary becomes more complex. On one hand students need to be taught not to be too dependent on vocabulary lists. On the other hand a good range of vocabulary is a critical part of second language acquisition.

Some words and expressions that are included in this book and the workbook are intended for recognition and comprehension rather than for formal learning. This applies to many 外来語「がいらいご」 used in the せいかつ and カタカナ sections of the workbook, and some footnoted items.

Vocabulary related to the main focus of the unit is presented towards the end of the unit. A variety of presentations has been used to avoid intimidating lists of words and expressions.

As with きもの 1 all vocabulary lists are arranged in the order of the Japanese syllabary chart, and Japanese-English and English-Japanese vocabulary lists appear at the end of the book.

せいかつ
The きもの course aims to integrate language studies with socio-cultural content.

The continuation from きもの 1 of the presentation of material via a series of letters from a young foreign student living in Japan is supplemented in きもの 2 by varying formats to introduce cultural insights. Some units present authentic brochures while others also present further cultural information in Japanese — this exposes students to the lifestyles of young people in modern Japan.

These sections can be used as starting points for further research or project work if desired. Exercises and ideas for follow-up activities are contained in the workbook and teacher's manual.

きもの 2 Workbook
The workbook accompanying the きもの 2 text contains a full range of exercises and activities which are designed to provide a thorough consolidation of the language points raised in the text. Its elements are outlined below:

ききましょう — listening comprehension exercises, the texts of which are spoken on the きもの 2 cassettes and written in the teacher's manual;

れんしゅうしましょう — contains a wide range of exercises and activities to provide mainly written reinforcement of the language content of each unit;

日本について — exercises and activities exploiting and extending the cultural material in each unit;

カタカナ — a comprehensive unit introducing the カタカナ script and reinforcing it via a variety of exercises and activities;

かんじ — the characters are given with their readings, definitions and stroke order. The readings given are those within the scope of the textbook.

きもの 2 Teacher's Manual
An invaluable resource for the teacher, this manual includes the elements below:

- the きもの method — an expanded discussion of points raised in this introduction;
- teacher's notes — how to use and exploit to the fullest all of the individual items in the course; how to use the course in class; sample lesson plans and guidelines for assessment;
- unit-by-unit analysis — includes a summary of the language presented, content of cassettes, suggestions for presenting each いいましょう exercise, scripts of listening comprehension activities, ideas for games and cultural units and some further language use explanations for teachers;
- reproduction masters — includes reading comprehension passages, sample tests for each unit and cartoon pages with separate listings of speech bubbles;
- photocopiable student progress sheets — provide students with the opportunity to assess positively their own progress.

きもの Cassettes
For each unit of the course, the cassettes contain:

- an entertaining recording of the まんが presented by young native Japanese speakers, both at normal speed and with pauses for repetition;
- a presentation of each いいましょう exercise;
- listening comprehension activities to accompany the ききましょう section of the きもの 2 workbook;
- a song and other items of interest in Japanese.

Acknowledgements

The publishers wish to thank the following organizations and people who contributed to the preparation of this book:

- The Japan Foundation Japanese Language Institute, for their generous financial support;
- Mr S. Kawate, Principal of the Noshiro North High School, for his cooperation and assistance;
- Dr and Mrs T. Kogure, Mr T. Sakaiya, the Ishida and Midorikawa families, Mr T. Matsuyama and Akiko Fujimori, for their assistance and hospitality;
- Katsuyuki Suzuki, Peter Burnham and Bill Farr for their general assistance;
- Toorak College, for its support.

The publishers also wish to acknowledge the following people who supplied photographs appearing in this book: Suzanne Burnham, Sumio Kawate, Sergio Montalban, Therese Hannan, Leanne Howard and Jacqui Beveridge.

Finally, the publishers gratefully acknowledge the companies who kindly gave their permission to use copyright material in this book. Despite every effort, the publishers were not always successful in tracing all copyright owners. Should this come to the attention of the copyright owners concerned, the publishers request that they contact them so that proper acknowledgement can be made in any reprint of this book.

第一課・おみやげ です。どうぞ。

いいましょう 一

 一  二  三

Using the example as a guide, talk about the pictures.

例:
> A ひまなとき なに を しますか。
> B Gitaa を ひきます。

 四  五  六

Using the example as a guide, talk about the pictures.

例:
> A ひまなとき なに を しますか。
> B Earobikusu を します。
>
> A どこ で?
> B たいいくかん で します。

Using the pictures as a guide, praise these people on their abilities.

例:
> A Erekutoon が じょうず ですね。
> B いいえ、そう でも ない です。

いいましょう 二

例:
どこ で たべましょうか。
ここ で たべましょう。

例:
どこ で たべましょうか。
そこ で たべましょう。

例:
どこ で たべましょうか。
あそこ で たべましょう。

例:
A どこ で たべましょうか。
B ここ で たべましょう。
　 or
　 そこ で たべましょう。
　 or
　 あそこ で たべましょう。

ともだちと

Make up a conversation with a partner.
Decide who will be A and who will be B.

| A | あっ、 | それは | おもしろい | T-shatsu とけい posutaa | ですね。 |

| B | そうですか。あたらしいです。 | Hawai やま Rokku-konsaato | でかいましたよ。 |

| A | だれと | Hawai やま Rokku-konsaato | にいきましたか。 |

| B | はは かぞく ともだち あね あに | といきました。 |

| A | Hawai やま Rokku-konsaato | で | すいえい saafin dansu saikuringu kyanpu | をしましたか。 |

| B | ええ、 | たのしかった つまらなかった よかった | です。 | [A]さん [A]くん | は | しゅうまつ やすみ にちようび | になにをしましたか。 |

| A | わたし ぼく | は | まち へや ともだちのうち にわ | で | famikonをしました。 CDをききました。 えいがをみました。 いぬとあそびました。 まんがをよみました。 |

いって みましょう

一 CD を どこで かいますか。

Where is the best place to buy CDs or jeans or hamburgers? Choose an item, such as one of the three above, and conduct a survey to find out where your classmates shop. Ask ten friends.

When you have completed your survey, you will be able to say which is the most popular shop among your friends.

Your survey form could look like this:

Survey on jiinzu	
なまえ	place
Robaato くん	Jeans City
Piitaa くん	Jac'n Jean
Maiku くん	Denim Heaven
Ben くん	Jac'n Jean

二 ひまなとき なに を しますか。

How well do you know your friend? Write down 6 statements (in 日本語 of course!) about what you think your friend does in her free time. She will also write down 6 statements. Ask her if she does what you have written. You can see how well you know her by the number of matching statements.

You may like to start by writing this:

Anさん は ひまなとき CD を ききます。　はい　いいえ

When you ask Anne, don't forget to put か on the end to make a question.

Here is a score sheet to check your friendship.

6	You know your friend very well.
5	You are good friends.
4	You know her quite well.
3	You have lots more to discover about your friend.
2	It should be fun getting to know her better!
1	Anne who?

三 じこしょうかい

じこしょうかい are used when you find yourself in a new situation and you need to introduce yourself. You might, like Maikuくん, be a new student to the class.

In Japan, じこしょうかい are used at school club meetings or scout meetings. They are also essential for writing to a pen-friend and for introducing yourself to new friends during a school visit or a home-stay. The content can vary according to the situation.

Listen to these students introducing themselves. You can use these examples to prepare a じこしょうかい for yourself.

ぼくの なまえは いわさき たけとし です。こうべに すんで います。 しょうがく 一ねんせい です。 ひまなとき こうえんで いぬと あそびます。 いぬが だいすき です。

わたしの なまえは ふじもり まりこ です。なごやに すんで います。いま 十四さいの ちゅうがく 二ねんせい です。おんがくが すき です。ピアノ が とくい です。ひまなとき ピアノ を ひきます。

わたしは いしだ ひさえ です。ひろしま に すんで います。わたしは こうこう 一ねんせい です。がっこうは おんがく の がっこう です。おんがくが だいすき です。ひまなとき ともだちの うちで CD を ききます。

ぼくは あまの ひでたか です。 とうきょうの しんじゅくに すんで います。ちゅうがく 一ねんせい です。 ぼくは supootsu が すき です。やきゅう が とくいです。ひまなとき ともだちと こうていで やきゅうを します。

単語 (たんご)

New words

あそこ	over there
あそびます	play, muck about
おみやげ	souvenir, present
おもしろい	fun, interesting
きょねん	last year
こうてい	school ground, oval
ここ	here
しょうかい (します)	introduce
しゅうまつ	weekend
すてきな	nice, lovely
せんしゅ	player, athlete
そこ	there
たいかい	contest
たいいくかん	gymnasium
だれ	who
とくい	I am good at...
とけい	clock, watch
ひきます	play stringed or keyboard musical instruments
へや	room

Expressions

あのこ、だれ?	Who is that kid?
あら?	Oh?!
うそ	That's a lie! I don't believe it!
おげんき ですか。	How are you?
かっこいい!	Cool! Far out!
すてき!	Gorgeous!
そうだ!	Oh, I know!
ちょうどいい	just right
…ですって	he/she says that...
ひまな とき	spare time, free time
ほんとうかなあ	I wonder if that's true.
やめて!	Cut it out! Stop that!

Schools and year levels

しょうがっこう	primary school
ちゅうがっこう	junior high school
こうとうがっこう (こうこう)	senior high school
しょうがく…ねんせい	primary school year level
ちゅうがく…ねんせい	junior high school year level
こうこう…ねんせい	senior high school year level

Katakana の 単語

earobikusu	aerobics
erekutoon	electric organ
ooru-sutaa	All Stars
gitaa	guitar
saafin	surfing
CD (shiidii)	CD
dansu	dance
chanpion	champion
T-shatsu (tii shatsu)	T-shirt
dizuniirando	Disneyland
Hawai	Hawaii
basuketto booru	basketball
famikon	home computer
piano	piano
rokku konsaato	rock music concert

第一課 九

せいかつ

3-21, Yukinoshita 1-chome,
Kamakura-shi, Kanagawa-ken,
Japan
15th September

Hi everyone,

I wasn't going to write until I got a letter from one of you, but at that rate you'll never hear from me again. Where have you all been? On holidays, I suppose. It would be nice to hear something occasionally, you know. A card, maybe?

Anyway, I just had to write to show you these latest photos. I bet you can't guess who this is.

Don't even try — it's Mr Tanaka. Old Mr Tanaka, that is, the one who lives in the house behind the one I live in. You know, you saw a picture of the inside last year.

Doesn't he look great? Guess how old — no, I'll tell you. He's 78. He's going through this really trendy phase. Well, here's a picture of him about twenty years ago, I think.

He was working for this company and then became a manager or a director or something. He just looks really ordinary, doesn't he? But now that he's old, he says that he doesn't have to worry about what people think or say any more. He can just do his own thing. Everyone looks up to old people here, and old Mr Tanaka is really taking advantage of it. If he does something a bit weird, they all say, 'That's OK, he's 78.' Talk about old people's liberation!

I'd better tell you where he is in the first photo. Well, the other day I noticed on the front seat of his car, and in the glove box, all these chocolate bars and sweets, so I asked him where he got them all. He said, 'Come with me,' and he took me to this huge, noisy, smoky place with all these sort of pinball machines. It's called a pachinko parlour. You could hear the music blaring out from it from about ten blocks away, no exaggeration. Pachinko parlours are really popular in Japan. Really popular!!! He told me to look as old as I could, because I don't think I'm supposed to be in there until I'm 18.

You have to try to get as many of these little metal balls out of the machines as you can, and then you go and cash them in. Except you don't get cash, you get cigarettes and sweets and things like that. Well, old Mr Tanaka has heaps of these things, which is funny, because he never eats them and he doesn't smoke. When he asked me what flavour sweets I wanted I said sutoroberii (you know what I mean, don't you?). Well, I'll never say that again. Old Mr Tanaka got really cross and started going on about all these new words coming in from English and taking over from proper Japanese words. 'What's wrong with いちご?' he kept asking. (That's the real word for 'strawberry'.) It's just that when you go to McDonald's or somewhere and ask for an いちご sheeku they'll probably say, 'You mean sutoroberii.' That's what happened when I asked for さくらんぼ and was told that it was cherii. I can see Mr Tanaka's point, really. It's not like he's really old-fashioned. He just wants to stop Japanese becoming full of these English-sounding words.

You should have heard him when Toshio brought him back a terehon kaado as おみやげ from his trip over the Seto Bridge. You need these telephone cards for most public phones in the cities now, and the ones with pictures on the back are popular as souvenirs and presents — especially the really cute ones. Well, Mr Tanaka liked the present, but hated the word terehon. He didn't mind kaado so much, but he said terehon was stupid, and much harder to say than でんわ.

Don't get the idea that Mr Tanaka is always grumbling. He's not. He's really happy. He keeps busy going back to visit the factory where he was the boss and taking an interest in how it's going. He says most Japanese people are a bit scared of retirement. He says it's important to keep working at something.

Well, anyway, his factory makes these dolls and he took me to see them being made. I'll never forget the women who sat there putting the finishing touches to the dolls.

All they had to do was paint in the eyes and mouth. They were just so quick and accurate, and they could look up and talk to Mr Tanaka without making a mistake. Mr Tanaka is really proud of these dolls. He said that really important people from other countries take them home as souvenirs of Japan. They'd make great おみやげ, I think. He said Prince Charles took one home. I bet he gave it to Princess Di.

Guess what!! Well, this is tomorrow, and Mr Tanaka has just given me a ticket for the big Madonna concert in とうきょう tonight. What a present! They cost about eighty or ninety dollars here, you know. Someone at his factory gave it to him. The only thing is, when I thanked him for the きっぷ for the konsaato he said that it wasn't a きっぷ but a chiketto. I knew that, but I was trying to keep old Mr Tanaka happy. You can't win. Anyway I bought him a terehon kaado with Madonna on it and told him to use it for his でんわ calls.

Must dash now. I've got a konsaato to get ready for. And you probably need to get on with some homework. I'm rapt in Madonna. She's so sensitive and the words of her songs just mean so much.

Lots of love,

Simone.

P.S. NOTE!!! My address is at the top of the letter...just in case you've lost it!

日本語 ノート

一 Complimenting and bragging

When you compliment someone, or they praise you, じょうず is used. This means 'You're good at...' To accept a compliment, because you are modest, it is usual to say 'いいえ、そう でもない です' which means 'No, not really.'

When you are talking to someone about your abilities, you must use とくい to mean 'I'm good at...'

e.g. ぼく は supootsu が とくい です。

However, as in English, you shouldn't brag too much.

二 Saying where you live

To ask someone where they live and to tell them where you live, you say,

どこ に すんで いますか。
Where do you live?
よこはま に すんで います。
I live in Yokohama.

When you talk about where you live and use すんで います, the place is followed by に.

三 Talking about your school year level
なんねんせい ですか。

In Japan, it is very common to ask students what year level they are. Sometimes people ask this instead of なんさい ですか。
To say which year level student you are, you say しょうがく or ちゅうがく or こうこう for the kind of school and then add your year level and ねんせい. To say that you were in third year of junior high, you would say ちゅうがく 三ねんせい です。

The words for primary school, junior high school and senior high school all end in がっこう, although a senior high school is usually called こうこう. This is an abbreviation of こうとうがっこう. But when you talk about your year level, you change しょうがっこう and ちゅうがっこう to しょうがく and ちゅうがく before adding ねんせい.

四 Saying where you do things — at/in a place

To say that you do something at a place, you say で after the place. Sometimes in English we say in a place (e.g. in the library, in the school ground). This is also で.

e.g. あした ともだち の うち で terebi を みます。
Tomorrow I'm going to watch TV at my friend's house.
どこ で かいましたか。
Where did you buy it?
Hawai で かいました。
I bought it in Hawaii.

五 Saying where you do things — here, there, over there

The words ここ, そこ, あそこ correspond to *here* or *this place*, *there* or *that place* and *over there*. When you use あそこ, you would usually point to the place as it is away, from both you and the person you are talking to.

e.g. ここ に きて ください。
Come here.
そこ で たべましょう。
Let's eat at that place.
あそこ で ともだち に あいました。
I met my friend over there.

六 Playing

In Japanese there are many words for 'play'. When you play (or do) a sport or game, you say します.

e.g. Badominton を します。

When you play a stringed or keyboard musical instrument, you usually say ひきます.

e.g. Piano を ひきます。

But if you just hang about with your friends or play around with the dog, you use あそびます.

e.g. いぬ と あそびます。

七 More about adjectives

In きもの Level 1, you learnt to comment on things using adjectives.

e.g. かわいい ですね。

You can also put adjectives before a noun or a word you want to describe, as you do in English. You have done this with:

e.g. いい おてんき ですね。
　　　It's a nice day, isn't it?

Here are some more examples:

あたらしい ともだち を
しょうかい します。
I'd like to introduce a new friend.
おもしろい おみやげ ですね。
What an interesting present!

八 ...ちゃん

...ちゃん is another form of address like ...さん and ...くん. But unlike ...さん and ...くん, ...ちゃん is never attached to a surname, only to a personal name or nickname. It is used to address small children and is also used by relatives and friends to address older girls.

がんばれ

Writing ひらがな

So, by now you have impressed all of your family and friends with your fantastic Japanese writing. But, deep down, you know that you still have some way to go before you can be fully satisfied with your ひらがな. Sometimes you look at a funny shape you have produced and realise that you have used an incorrect stroke order. At other times you realise that things are out of balance because the length of the strokes is not quite right.

But don't despair! Of course you need to keep working on your ひらがな! After all, your beautiful English handwriting was not something you mastered in just one year. Actually, Japanese children keep special 'doriru' books to practise their writing in. That's not a bad idea, is it?

Whether you choose to do that or not, you will need to make improving your ひらがな one of the goals for your second level of Japanese study. In the end, you will know that you have acquired a really special skill.

おめでとう!

You are now able to use your 日本語 to:

- introduce yourself
- ask where someone lives
- tell someone where you live
- find out what year level someone is in at school
- say what year level you are
- ask what someone does in their spare time
- ask and tell people where activities happen
- give and accept compliments

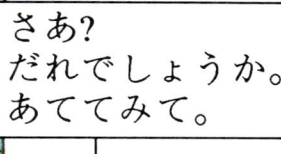

いいましょう 一

Using the example as a guide, comment on the people in the drawing.
The expressions given in the box may be of use.

例:

A このひとは せがたかい ですね。
  だれ ですか。
B Kenくん です。

めが おおきい
せが たかい
せが ひくい
かみが ながい
かみが みじかい

おかあさんは せがひくい
ですね。じゅんいちくんは
せがたかい ですね。

いいましょう 二

一 hansamu な ひと
　ゆうめい な ひと
　いや な ひと

二 きれい な ひと
　しずか な ひと
　ゆうめい な ひと

三 へん な ひと
　いや な ひと
　すてき な ひと

 ①
 ③
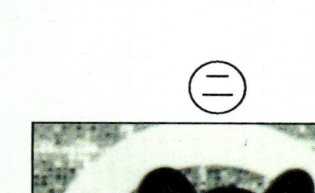 ②

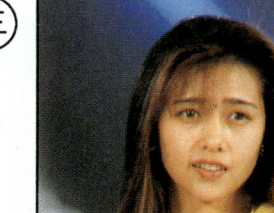
 ④
 ⑤

Using the examples as a guide, comment on the pictures.

例:
A hansamu な ひと ですね。
B そう ですね。
　or
　そう ですか。

例:
A この ひと は hansamu ですね。
B そう ですね。
　or
　そう ですか。

いいましょう 三

- かお を あらって います。
- すうがく を べんきょう して います。
- でんしゃ を まって います。
- 本 を よんで います。
- まんが を かいて います。

一

二

三

四

五

六

Look at the pictures and ask your partner what each person is doing.

例:
A この ひと は いま なに を して (い)ますか。
B かお を あらって (い)ます。

いいましょう 四

Invite someone to share in these activities.
They may accept or decline.

例:
> A きょう じょうば に いきませんか。
> B ええ、いい ですね。
>   or
>   じょうば ですか。じょうば は ちょっと…

You may suggest another activity.

例:
> A きょう じょうば に いきませんか。
> B じょうば ですか。じょうば は ちょっと…
> A じゃ、saikuringu は?
> B ええ、いい ですよ。

You may arrange a better time.

例:
> A きょう じょうば に いきませんか。
> B きょう は ちょっと…
> A じゃ、あした は?
> B あした ですか。ええ、いい ですよ。

ともだちと

Make up a conversation with a partner.
Decide who will be A and who will be B.

A: [B]さん、/[B]くん、 なに を して いますか。

B: しゃしん を みて います。

A: しゃしん ですか。みせて ください。

B: どうぞ。

A: あっ、ねこ の しゃしん ですね。とても / へんな / きれいな / おもしろい ねこ ですね。

みみ が ながい / め が おおきい / あし が みじかい ですね。この ねこ は なに を して いますか。

B: あ、Buronson は terebi を みて います。/ CD を きいて います。/ booru あそび を して います。 terebi / booru あそび / おんがく が だいすき です。

ねえ、[A]さん、/[A]くん、あした あたらしい CD を ききませんか。/ basuketto booru を しませんか。/ うみ に いきませんか。/ bideo を みませんか。

A: あした は ちょっと...

B: じゃ、らいしゅう の どようび / にちようび は?

A: どようび / にちようび ですか。いい ですよ。

いってみましょう

Pururu-pururu...Ringing up

There are several ways of making telephone calls. Here are two patterns.

たけしくん is ringing the やまだ house to talk to his friend, たろうくん. Mr やまだ answers the phone.

1 やまださん: もしもし。
　たけし: もしもし。やまださん の おたく ですか。
　やまださん: はい、そう です。
　たけし: たけし です。あのう、たろうくん おねがい します。
　やまださん: はい、ちょっと まってください。

2 たろう: もしもし。やまだ です。
　たけし: ああ、たろうくん。たけし です。

At the end of your call, you can say じゃあね, an informal way of saying 'goodbye' which should be used only with people you know well.

Now it's your turn. Ring up a friend. His or her mother answers the phone so you have to ask for your friend. Invite your friend to go somewhere or to participate in an activity with you. This friend is not keen on what you suggest so arrange to go somewhere else. Also, the time you suggest is inconvenient for your friend so try to arrange a time to suit you both. You will need to arrange where and at what time you will meet and then ring off.

せいかつ

A letter from Simone.

みなさん へ、
おげんきですか。わたしは げんきです。
日本語で、てがみを かきます！
　きのう、すてきな スコットくんと、ジョギングに いきました。たのしかったです。スコットくんは、とても ハンサムな ひとです。せが たかくて、あたまが いいです。わたしも、あたまが いいですね。ハハハ！
　スコットくんの いぬも、ジョギングに ついて きました。いぬの なまえは、サシャです。サシャは、めが おおきいです。スコットくんも、めが おおきいです。
　いま、はるこちゃんは、まんがを みています。はるこちゃんは、まんがが だいすきです。としおくんは、にわで おとうさんと、ボールあそびを しています。おかあさんは、えいごを べんきょうしています。おかあさんは、べんきょうが すきです。へんな ひとですね。
　はやく てがみを かいてください。まっています。
　バイバイ。
　　　　　　　　　　　シモーンより
　　　　　日よう日の ごごの 二じ。
P.S. この レター・ペーパーは、かわいいですね。

へ	to
たか<u>くて</u>	tall <u>and</u>
ついて	follow
より	from

日本語 ノート

一 Describing yourself and others

In きもの 1, when you learnt to say who likes something, you said

はなこさん は おかし が すき です。
Hanako likes sweets.

You can use this same pattern to describe how someone looks.

e.g. Teriiくん は せ が たかい です。
Terry is tall.
Chappiiちゃん は あし が ながい です。
Chappy has long legs.
Dambo は みみ が おおきい です。
Dumbo has big ears.

This pattern is also used to describe how intelligent someone is.

e.g. Amandaさん は あたま が いい です。
Amanda is clever.

二 More about describing

You know lots of good words to describe things.

e.g. つまらない　むずかしい
　　 ちいさい　　あたらしい

All of these adjectives end with い, so we call them い adjectives. There is another group of adjectives that doesn't end in い (e.g. いや, しずか) — these are called な adjectives because when they are followed directly by a noun, な has to be included.

e.g. いやな しゃしん ですね。
What a horrible photo!

If you are not using a noun directly after the adjective, then な is not used.

e.g. この しゃしん は いや ですね。
This photo is horrible, isn't it?

There are some exceptions to the rule about い adjectives: even though きれい and ゆうめい end in い, they are な adjectives. You must put な after them when a noun follows directly.

e.g. きれいな きもの ですね。
Isn't that a pretty kimono.

ゆうめいな みせ で かいました。
She bought it at a famous shop.

三 Agreeing and disagreeing

Note that when you say そう ですね, you are agreeing with your friend's comment. If you don't really agree, you can say そう ですか with a rising tone.

四 Inviting people out

When you want to invite people to do things or go to places, you use the ...ませんか ending on verbs. In 日本語 you are really asking 'Won't you ...?' Of course, in English we usually say 'Would you like to...'

e.g. きょう かいもの に いきませんか。
Would you like to go shopping today?

If you really enjoy shopping, you'd accept the invitation by saying,

ええ、いい ですね。
Yeah, that'd be good.

If you are not that keen on shopping, you could say,

かいもの ですか。かいもの は ちょっと...
Shopping? I don't really like shopping...

and when your friend suggests something better, you can then accept by saying,

ええ、いい ですよ。
Yes, that sounds good.

If you'd like to go, but can't go today, you say,

きょう は ちょっと...
Today is not very good for me...

You can then work out a more suitable time. Note that sometimes a question repeating the activity or time is used.

e.g. A あした じょうば に いきませんか。
　　 B じょうば ですか。じょうば は ちょっと...

This is to confirm what you heard, or you may use it just to give you some extra time to think.

五　て form of verbs

You have already met many examples of verbs in て form.

e.g. かして、すわって、きいて

Think of て as a base form of the verb. When you add words to the base form you get other meanings. If you add ください, it becomes a request.

e.g. けし gomu を かして ください。
ここ に きて ください。

If you add います to the て form, it tells you what someone is doing now.

e.g. たけしくん は いま なに を して いますか。
What is Takeshi doing?
Terebi を みて います。
He's watching TV.

When you hear Japanese people speaking, you'll hear that they shorten て います to て ます.

e.g. 日本語 を べんきょう して (い)ます。
I'm studying Japanese.
本 を よんで (い)ます。
He's reading a book.

Because て form is a base form, you need to know how to form it. This chart of verbs, which you already know, shows that how you form the て base form depends on what kind of verb you are dealing with and what comes before ます.

You will notice that a couple of groups end in で instead of て but we still call this the て form. The て form is a complex form and you probably will find it difficult at first. But, like most things in 日本語, it looks harder than it really is!

ーます form	て form
WEAK	
あけます しめます たべます みせます みます	あけて しめて たべて みせて みて
STRONG	
すわります	すわって
あいます あらいます いいます かいます	あって あらって いって かって
たちます まちます	たって まって
かきます ききます ひきます	かいて きいて ひいて
あそびます	あそんで
のみます よみます	のんで よんで
かします	かして
IRREGULAR	
いきます きます します	いって きて して

おめでとう！

You are now able to use your 日本語 to:

- describe people and things
- invite friends out
- accept and decline an invitation
- say what people are doing at this moment
- get a friend to the phone when you ring

単語 (たんご)

New words

い adjectives

たかい	high, expensive
ながい	long
ひくい	low
みじかい	short

な adjectives

いや	horrible, terrible
きれい	pretty, clean
しずか	quiet
すてき	nice, wonderful
hansamu	good-looking, handsome
へん	strange
ゆうめい	famous

Expressions

あててみて	have a guess
ーありがとう ございます	thank you very much
おいで	come here (calling a dog)
ーおねがい します	may I have...?
そんなに (たかくない)	not that (tall)
だれ でしょうか	who do you think?

ーえ	picture, painting
ーおたく	your house
ーか	or
かきます	write, draw
ーこの ひと	this person, he/she
ーしゃしん	photograph
ーしんぶん	newspaper
ーとても	very
とっても	very!
ーべんきょう します	study
ーひと	person
ーbooru あそび	playing with a ball

Parts of the body

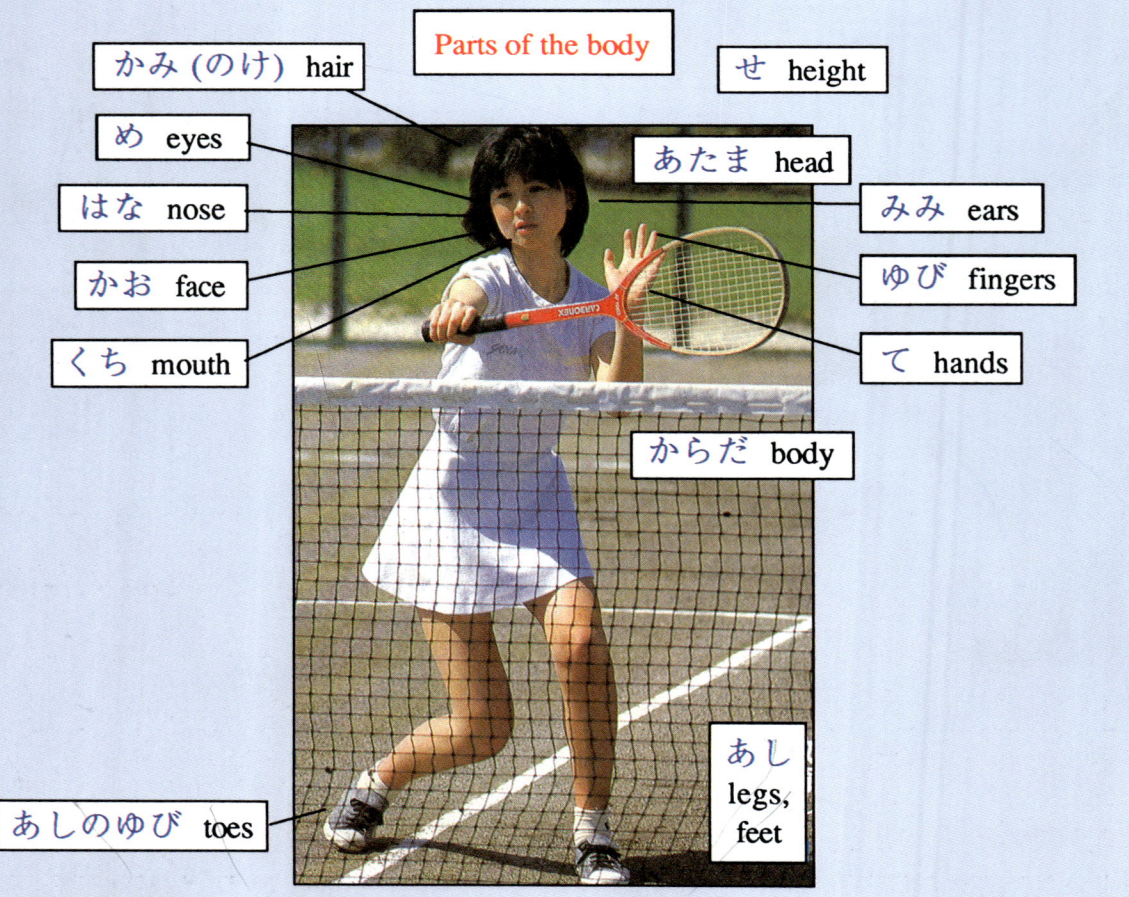

- かみ (のけ) hair
- め eyes
- はな nose
- かお face
- くち mouth
- せ height
- あたま head
- みみ ears
- ゆび fingers
- て hands
- からだ body
- あし legs, feet
- あしのゆび toes

カタカナ

As you know, ordinary written Japanese uses a mixture of *hiragana*, *kanji* and *katakana*.

Katakana is used mainly for words and names borrowed from other languages. Since most *katakana* words are derived from English, they are easy to understand, e.g. tenisu (テニス), basu (バス), hotto doggu (ホット ドッグ). However, there are many borrowed words which have been shortened or changed so that they no longer seem like English words, e.g. famikon (ファミコン).

Katakana is used for some Japanese words. These include noise words (e.g. wan wan ワン ワン for a dog's bark), baby talk, slang, technical words, company names and nicknames. *Katakana* is also sometimes used in the same way as we use *italics*, to make something stand out visually. Below is the katakana chart.

	A	I	U	E	O
	ア	イ	ウ	エ	オ
K	カ	キ	ク	ケ	コ
G	ガ	ギ	グ	ゲ	ゴ
S	サ	シ	ス	セ	ソ
Z	ザ	ジ	ズ	ゼ	ゾ
T	タ	チ	ツ	テ	ト
D	ダ	(ヂ) (ji)	(ヅ) (zu)	デ	ド
N	ナ	ニ	ヌ	ネ	ノ
H	ハ	ヒ	フ	ヘ	ホ
B	バ	ビ	ブ	ベ	ボ
P	パ	ピ	プ	ペ	ポ
M	マ	ミ	ム	メ	モ
Y	ヤ		ユ		ヨ
R	ラ	リ	ル	レ	ロ
W	ワ				ヲ (o)
N	ン (n)				

Look closely at the カタカナ chart. The most obvious difference between カタカナ and ひらがな is that the カタカナ letters have sharp angles and straighter lines. Although this makes the letters easier to write, it does not lessen the task of learning them all! You probably had some good ways for learning ひらがな. You can use many of these to help you remember カタカナ. Here are some further hints:

- There are several カタカナ that look like their ひらがな equivalent, e.g. カ (か), キ (き) and ヘ (へ). ニ look like かんじ 二.

- As you did with ひらがな, see if you can see a picture in each letter that will help you remember the sound. Can you see ro (ロ), for robotto (ロボット) in the illustration below?

- There are some groups of similar-looking カタカナ, e.g. ツ tsu, ソ so, ノ no. One way to remember these is to make up some reminders. For example, you could say that tsu (ツ) has tsu (two) small strokes, no (ノ) has no small strokes and so (ソ) is the sole letter with one stroke.

Unfortunately there are no short-cuts to learning カタカナ. As you discovered when you learnt ひらがな, what is really necessary is some hard work! However, once you have learnt to read カタカナ you will be able to expand your vocabulary very quickly as most カタカナ words are easy to remember. Many signs and menus in Japan are written in カタカナ and when you visit Japan, you'll be surprised at how much you can read.

Writing カタカナ

You will be doing lots of writing practice in your *Workbook* but first let's look at the similarities and differences between spelling rules in カタカナ and in ひらがな.

Little tsu ッ

Just as in ひらがな when little つ is used to double the sound of the consonant that follows (e.g. すわって), little ッ in カタカナ does the same.

e.g.   ペット   petto
         キッス   kissu
         トラック   torakku

Little ya ャ , yu ュ, yo ョ

Little ャ, ョ, ュ combine in the same way as they did in ひらがな to make a new sound.

	ャ	ュ	ョ
キ	キャ	キュ	キョ
ギ	ギャ	ギュ	ギョ
シ	シャ	シュ	ショ
ジ	ジャ	ジュ	ジョ
チ	チャ	チュ	チョ
ニ	ニャ	ニュ	ニョ
ヒ	ヒャ	ヒュ	ヒョ
ビ	ビャ	ビュ	ビョ
ピ	ピャ	ピュ	ピョ
ミ	ミャ	ミュ	ミョ
リ	リャ	リュ	リョ

Examples of words using these sounds are:

   T シャツ   T-shatsu
   ジュニア   junia
   ジョギング   jogingu

Making double vowel sounds

In ひらがな, as you know, there are two ways of making double vowel sounds. One is to repeat the vowel as in おかあさん and おにいさん and おねえさん. The other rule is for double お sounds when the double お is written with う as in おとうさん and おはよう.

When writing in カタカナ, this double vowel sound is written as a bar.

e.g.　スポーツ　supootsu
　　　ギター　　gitaa
　　　ニュース　nyuusu
　　　ケーキ　　keeki

When writing vertically, the bar becomes vertical too.

e.g.　スポーツ　ギター　ニュース　ケーキ

Making new sounds

There are some sound combinations that have been created just to write foreign words. Sounds like *fa*, *fi*, *che*, *di* are sounds that do not exist in Japanese words. These new sounds are written using little ア, イ, エ, オ and ユ. (See below.)

ア	クァ kwa	グァ gwa				ツァ tsa		ファ fa
イ							ティ ti	ディ di	フィ fi
エ			シェ she	ジェ je	チェ che	ツェ tse		フェ fe
オ	クォ kwo					ツォ tso		フォ fo
ユ							デュ dyu	

カタカナ 三十

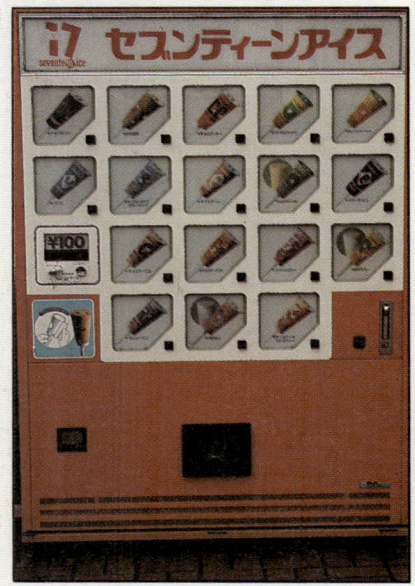

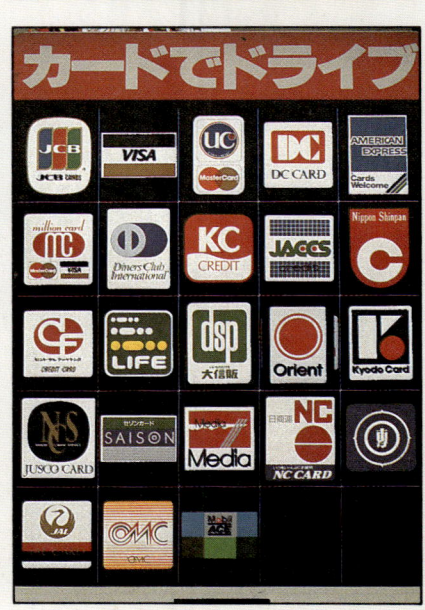

いいましょう 一

Using the pictures as a guide, talk about what is wrong with you.

例:
A どうしたん です か。
B おなか が いたいん です。

いいましょう 二

Using the example as a guide, talk about where the scouts and guides are from.

例:
> A ひでおくん は どこ から きましたか。
> B 日本 から きました。

Using the example as a guide, talk about what language (or languages) the scouts and guides speak.

例:
> A ひでおくん は なに語 を はなしますか。
> B 日本語 と えい語 を はなします。

Using the example as a guide, talk about the nationalities of the scouts and guides.

例:
> A ひでおくん は ちゅうごく人 ですか。
> B いいえ、日本人 です。

いいましょう 三

おいしいですね。

いいえ、おいしくないです。

一 おもしろいですね。
二 むずかしいですね。
三 きたないですね。
四 おいしいですね。
五 ちいさいですね。
六 あついですね。

Listen to the example below, look at the pictures and respond with what you imagine the other person is saying.

例:
A おもしろいですね。
B いいえ、おもしろくないです。

しずか ですね。

① しずか ですね。

② いや ですね。

③ きれい ですね。

④ へん ですね。

⑤ ゆうめい ですね。

Listen to the example below, look at the pictures and respond with what you imagine the other person is saying.

例:
A しずか ですね。
B いいえ、しずか じゃない です。

てんき

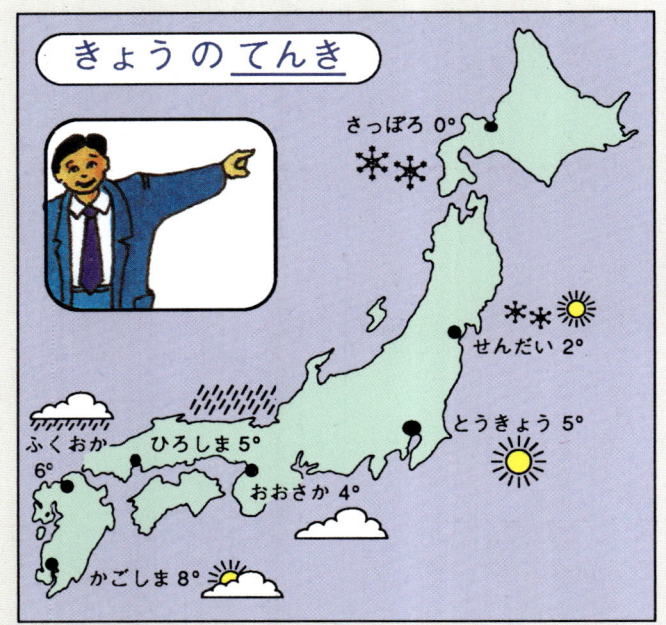
きょうの てんき

あしたの てんき

☀	fine	はれ でしょう	it will be fine
☁	cloudy	くもり でしょう	it will be cloudy
🌧	rain	あめ でしょう	it will rain
❄	snow	ゆき でしょう	it will snow
⛅	fine/cloudy	はれ のち くもり でしょう	it will be fine; cloudy later
🌥	cloudy/rain	くもり のち あめ でしょう	it will be cloudy; rain later
🌦	rain/fine	あめ のち はれ でしょう	it will rain; fine later
❄☀	snow/fine	ゆき のち はれ でしょう	it will snow; fine later

Talk about the weather today and tomorrow in the city of your choice.

A とうきょうの てんき は どう ですか。
B はれ です。
A 何ど ですか。
B 5ど です。
A あした は どう でしょうか。
B あめ でしょう。

てんき － weather　でしょう － it will be　のち － later　ど － degrees

ともだちと

Make up a conversation with a partner.
Decide who will be A and who will be B.

がっこうで

| A | [B]さん、[B]くん、 | ひろしくん ミシェルさん マリオくん (アンさん) | は | らいしゅう | 日本 フランス イタリア イギリス | にかえりますね。 |

| | きょう (あした) どようびに | おみやげを かいましょうか。 |

| B | ええ、そう しましょう。 |

デパートで

| B | あっ、この | おんがく ビデオ とけい 本 | を | きいて みて | ください。 | おもしろい いい きれい すてき | ですね。 |

| A | えっ？そう ですか。 | (おもしろくない) よくない きれいじゃない すてきじゃない | ですよ。 |

| | とても | うるさい へんな (つまらない) | おんがく ビデオ とけい 本 | です。これは どう ですか。 |

| B | それは ちょっと...。 | ひろしくん ミシェルさん マリオくん アンさん | は | ファミコンを しますか。 まんがを よみますか。 えを かきますか。 テニスを しますか。 |

| A | ええ、 | します。 よみます。 かきます。 |

| B | じゃ、 | ファミコン ゲーム
まんが
かみ と クレヨン
テニス の 本 | を かいましょうか。 |

| A | あ、それ は いい ですね。 |

いってみましょう

いいえ...

You have a friend who is great company but is really lazy. No matter what you suggest doing, this friend always has an excuse for not going along with you.

You have to come up with as many suggestions or invitations as possible about where to go and what to do. Try to persuade your friend by telling him or her that it will be fun or easy. Your classmate, who is role-playing your friend, has to think up as many excuses as possible for not going to these places or for not doing these things.

Here are some examples to get you going.

Suggestion/invitation	Excuse
サイクリング に いきませんか。 ハンバーガー を たべましょうか。 サッカー を しましょうか。 ボール あそび を しませんか。	サイクリング は ちょっと... ハンバーガー は あんまり... あし が いたいん です。 ボール あそび は おもしろくない です。

You know you have won the day when your friend runs out of excuses.

ローラー スケート を しませんか。

日本語 ノート

一 It hurts...!

The Japanese word for *ouch!* or *it hurts!* is いたい. When you want to explain what part of your body is sore, you use the following expression:

...が いたいん です。

So, if a headache is the reason you can't do the test scheduled for today, you'd look pained and say,

あたま が いたいん です。

If you have a sore throat, you can suffer in silence or say,

のど が いたいん です。

To find out what the matter with someone is, you ask,

どうしたん ですか。

二 Coming and going

When you invite someone to come to your house, you use the verb きます (*come*), but when they accept, they use いきます (*go*).

e.g. ようこさん、ぼく の うち に きませんか。
Yoko, will you come to my place?
ええ、いきます。
Yes, I'll come.

You could say that ええ、いきます means *Yes, I'll go (to your house)*.

いきます is always used when you go somewhere else. When you talk about someone coming to where you are, you must use きます.

Another use of きます is found in the expression どこから きましたか。 This means *Where do you come from?* and is used to ask someone's country of birth.

三 Returning home

When you ask someone when they are going home, you use the verb かえります (*go home, return*).

e.g. いつ うち に かえりますか。
When are you going home?

If someone is going back to their country, they will also use かえります. Someone who lives in アメリカ might tell you,

らいげつ アメリカ に かえります。
I'm going back to America next month.

四 Some more set expressions

By now, you've probably realized that Japanese has many set expressions that you are required to use in given situations. When you are a visitor to a friend's house, you say おじゃま します as you enter. When you leave, you say おじゃま しました. While this expression means *I'm in your way*, you can think of it as meaning *Thank you for having me*.

There are also expressions and responses that are used when people leave their own house and when they arrive back home. You probably remember these from きもの 1.

五 It's not difficult! It's not strange!

You already know that when you want to say that something is difficult, you say むずかしい です. If you want to say that it is not difficult, you say むずかしくない です.

Another example is,

おおきい です ね。　It's big, isn't it?
おおきくない です。　It isn't big.

The only exception to this pattern for い adjectives is いい, which doesn't have a negative form. Fortunately there is another word, よい, which means *good* or *nice* and it does have a negative form, よくない. So, you might hear people disagreeing by saying,

いい です ね。
That's good, isn't it?
よくない です。
It's not good.

If you want to say that something (or someone) is strange, you say へん です. If you want to say that it is not strange, you say,

へんじゃない です.

Another example is,

きれい です ね。
It's pretty, isn't it?
きれい じゃない です。
It's not pretty.

There are no exceptions to this pattern for な adjectives.

単語 (たんご)

Country	Nationality -人	Language -語
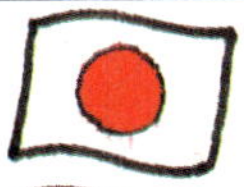 日本	日本人	日本語
 ちゅうごく	ちゅうごく人	ちゅうごく語
 アメリカ	アメリカ人	えい語
 イギリス	イギリス人	えい語
 イタリア	イタリア人	イタリア語
 インドネシア	インドネシア人	インドネシア語
 オーストラリア	オーストラリア人	えい語
 カナダ	カナダ人	えい語、フランス語
 ニュージーランド	ニュージーランド人	えい語
 ドイツ	ドイツ人	ドイツ語
 フランス	フランス人	フランス語
 メキシコ	メキシコ人	スペイン語

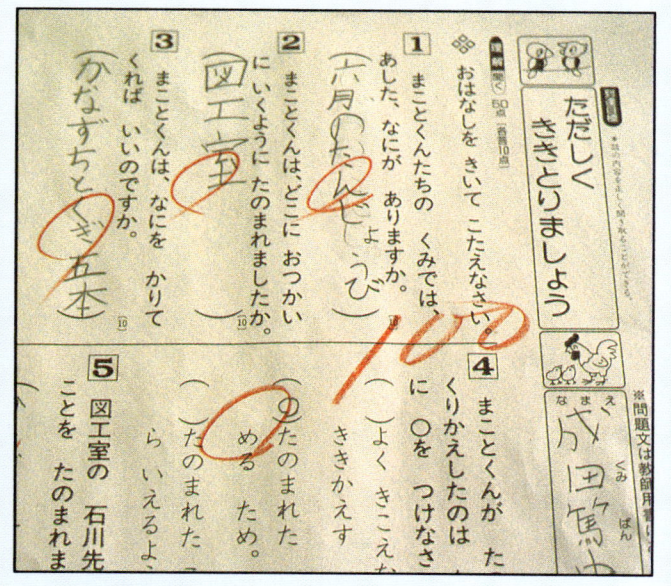

Imagine that you have received this piece of corrected work back from your teacher. You might be anxious about the red circles called まる. Perhaps you would be reassured by the 100 and the teacher's comment of よくできました *Well done!* In Japan, まる represents correct work like a tick, whereas ばつ means wrong or incorrect. ばつ is written as X.

New words and expressions

かえります	— return, go home
はなします	— speak
もう	— already

おみまい Visiting someone who is sick

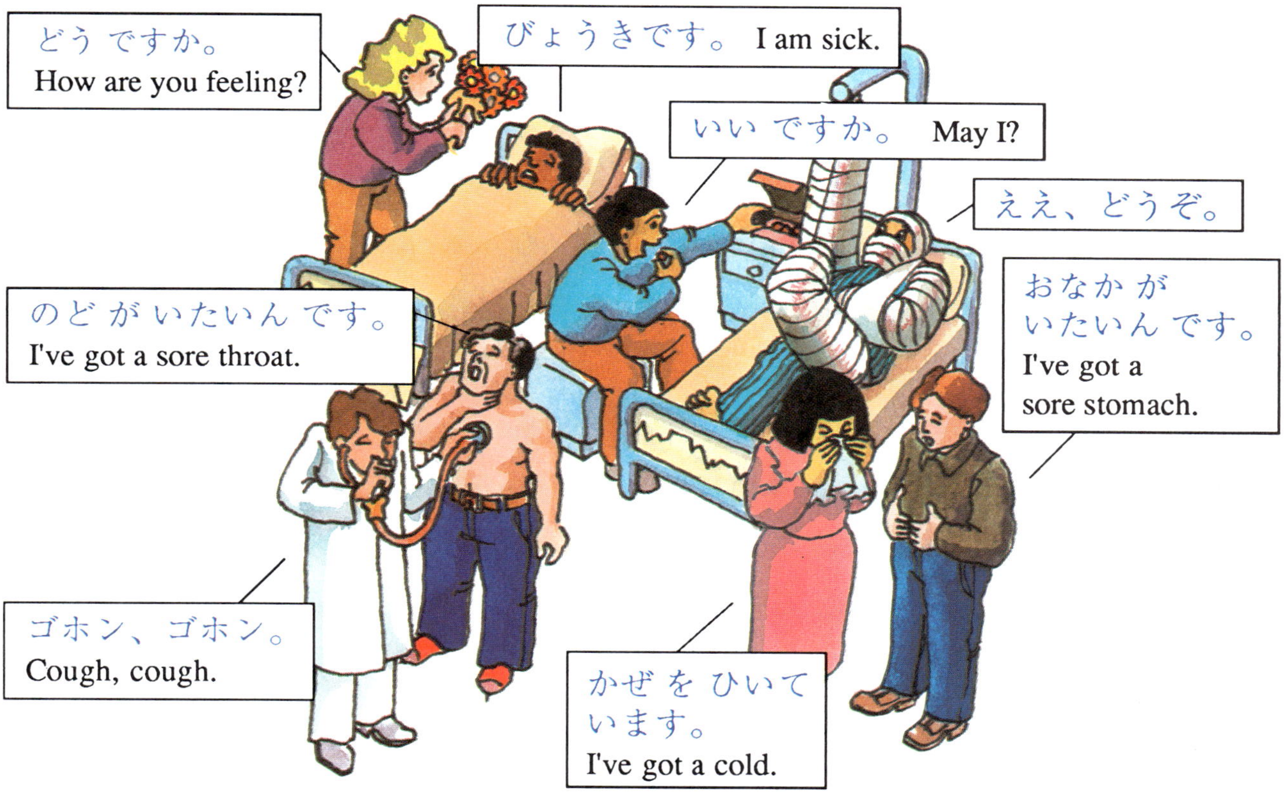

どう ですか。 How are you feeling?

びょうき です。 I am sick.

いい ですか。 May I?

ええ、どうぞ。

のど が いたいんです。 I've got a sore throat.

おなか が いたいんです。 I've got a sore stomach.

ゴホン、ゴホン。 Cough, cough.

かぜ を ひいて います。 I've got a cold.

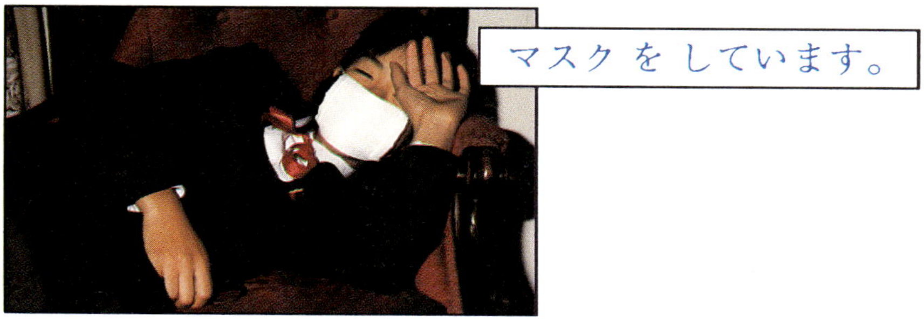

マスク を しています。

せいかつ

Meet ゆきこ and えつこ, two young office ladies with the Mitsubishi Bank in とうきょう. They both started working there at the beginning of last year and have become very good friends. Now they are nearing the end of their second year with the bank, and most of their lunchtime conversations are about one thing: their annual holidays. They plan to take them in just over a month's time.

ゆきこ and えつこ were still at university when Japanese workers only got two weeks' annual leave. Now nearly everyone gets three weeks and more and more young people plan to 'go away' for most of that time.

Fortunately, they earn very good wages and most young people like ゆきこ and えつこ find it fairly easy to save. Both of them still live at home so they don't have to worry about big living expenses like food and rent. えつこ was thinking of buying a car, but, as ゆきこ pointed out, she has nowhere at home to keep it and the traffic in and around the city makes driving far too difficult. So, all they have to spend their money on is clothes — expensive clothes, mind you, and always with designer labels. And ゆきこ, especially, spends quite a bit on music. She has the latest pop CDs from all over the world. But that still leaves quite a bit to spend on their holidays, and the Japanese government really encourages people to spend some of their savings.

So where to this year? Well, both of them have already been to Europe. えつこ was given a trip to London, Paris and Rome as a graduation present at the end of her university course. ゆきこ went there at the end of her first year with the bank. It was a group holiday organised by the bank, and she still has sixty-two group photos to prove it. And えつこ still has the perfume in the Eiffel Tower bottle that her friend brought back as おみやげ. So when they look at the Europe brochures and schedules, it's more a case of nostalgia than practical planning.

What about somewhere exotic, like Australia? And Hawaii looks かわいい. But every time えつこ suggests one of these places, ゆきこ tries to change the subject. Eventually she admits that she is reserving one of them for her honeymoon.

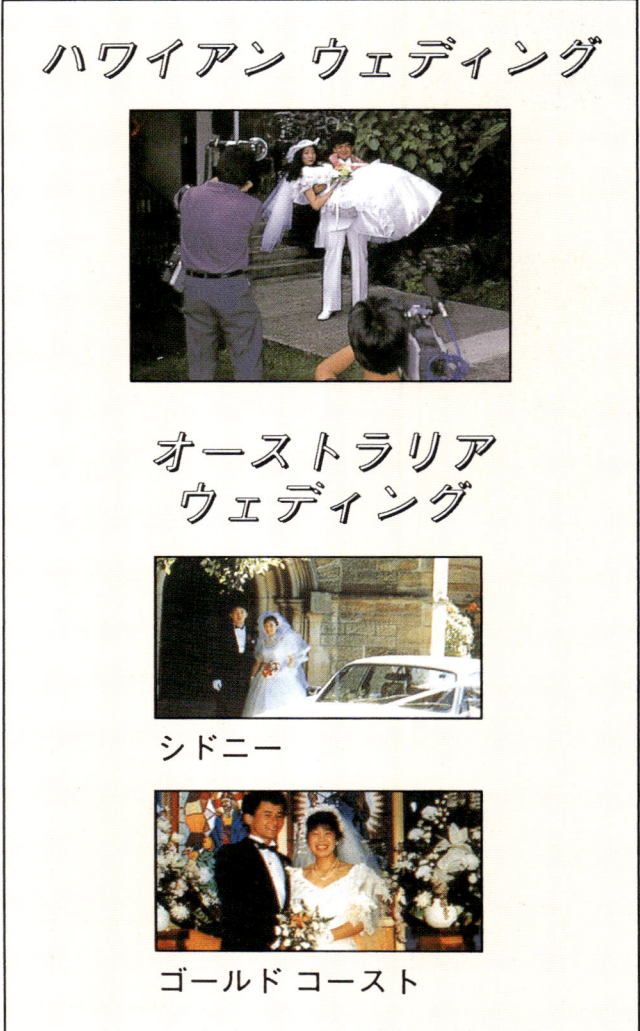

What they need now is something new and exciting, a new experience. After all, they seem to lead highly organized lives. Even their leisure time seems full of discipline. ゆきこ has been going to tea ceremony classes for about 18 months now, and progress seems so slow. She enjoys it, but sometimes she feels she will never really master it. えつこ feels much the same way about her flower arranging class.

And so they reach a decision. They will go on one of the holiday packages in Japan offering to teach them a new skill in just a few days. So, what will it be? Horse riding? Tennis? Scuba diving?

ゆきこ doesn't mind which one it is, as long as it has おんせん. おんせん are hot springs and the natural hot water is piped into big baths. At the resort hotels おんせん baths often overlook the sea or a valley. Some are outdoors and ゆきこ went to one in winter where she soaked in an outdoor hot pool surrounded by snow. As ゆきこ says, a relaxing おんせん could be just what is needed after a day on horseback.

スクーバダイビング

イントロダクトリースペシャル			
日何		プレイ	ホテル
1	ANA ✈ ホテル 🚌	フリータイム	オーシャンビューホテル
2	ダイビング・フリータイム	午前 a.m.: スクーバ・ダイビング1日1ダイブ (タンク1本) 午後 p.m.: オプショナル・ダイビング	オーシャンビューホテル
3	ホテル 🚗 ANA ✈	フリータイム	

テニススクール

アスレジャークラブ

🎾 レンタルテニス　♨ おんせん　⛳ ゴルフ
🚲 レンタルサイクル　👟 レジャーランド　🏊 プール

スケジュール		
1	JR - 11.30 🚃 13.00 - 17.00 20.00 - 21.00	ウエルカム ドリンク (コーヒー or ティー) レッスン VTR による ミーティング
2	9.00 - 12.00 13.00 - 17.00 19.00 - 21.00	レッスン レッスン パーティー
3	9.30 - 12.00 14.00 - 16.00 17.00	レッスン フリータイム JR 🚃

乗馬(じょうば)スクール

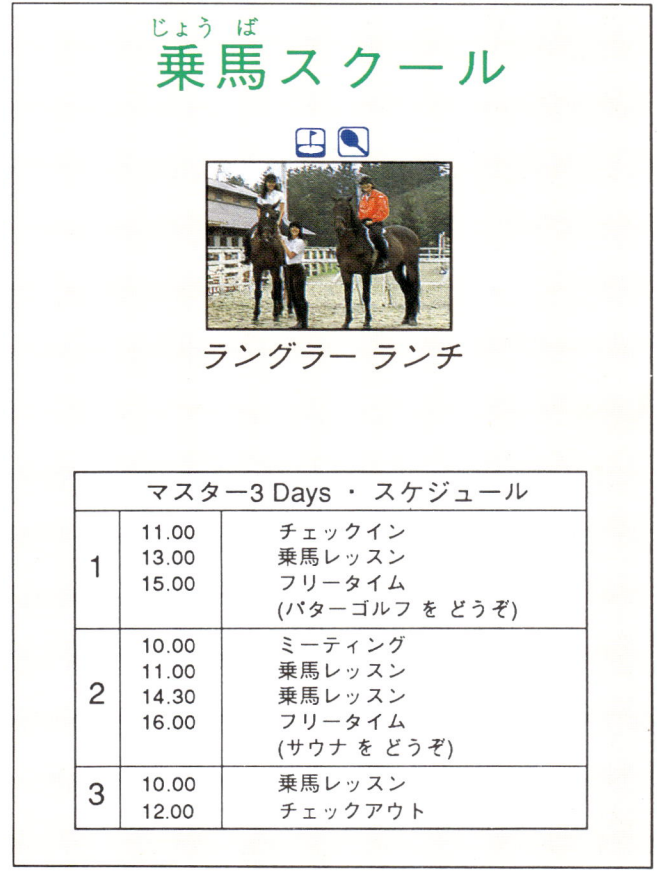

ラングラー ランチ

マスター3 Days・スケジュール		
1	11.00 13.00 15.00	チェックイン 乗馬レッスン フリータイム (パターゴルフ をどうぞ)
2	10.00 11.00 14.30 16.00	ミーティング 乗馬レッスン 乗馬レッスン フリータイム (サウナ をどうぞ)
3	10.00 12.00	乗馬レッスン チェックアウト

がんばれ

Learning the words

One thing that should be clear to you by now is that attending classes is only part of what is required of you as a language learner. Just being 'there' is not enough! No matter how many lively activities you take part in, you still need to find some quiet learning times of your own so that you can master the new words and expressions that you are meeting. You sometimes hear people complain that they learn the たんご but forget everything the next day. That's because they don't know these helpful hints for vocabulary learning.

1 For every word that you are learning, make up a personal memory system that ensures that you won't forget it. The best way is to use sound and image association. Take the word きたない, for example. Don't just read it, say it out loud, and say it 'dirty'. That -ない ending on the word makes it easy to say it with a filthy, grimy feeling. Think 'dirty' while you say it: piles of greasy dishes or muddy sneakers on white carpet. The word きれい, on the other hand, is just right for saying in a light, 'pretty' way. You will never forget しずか if you concentrate on the first sound as you say it.

These memory aids may sound silly, but that's the whole point. The sillier your personal system is, the more likely it is that you will remember the words.

2 Don't just run your eye up and down the word lists a couple of times. Get busy with a pen and paper. Write words down (this will help your ひらがな writing too), especially the ones that you keep getting wrong. Test yourself by covering first one side of the たんご, then the other.

3 Divide and conquer. Set yourself realistic targets. Don't attempt to learn a whole page at a time, but take advantage of the fact that your きもの word lists are divided into convenient, manageable sections.

4 It takes two to たんご. Get someone else involved in your vocabulary learning. Ask a family member to 'hear' you. They probably won't know if you are wrong or right, but you will, and that's the most important thing. You can arrange to have a たんご partner at school — agree to test each other regularly.

Whatever method you choose, remember it's up to you. You can't just expect to absorb all the Japanese you need to know just by being there.

おめでとう

You are now able to use your 日本語 to:

- find out what is wrong with someone
- describe your aches and pains
- describe things and people
- talk about people's nationalities and what language they speak
- be a polite visitor
- read lots of country names in カタカナ
- talk about the weather

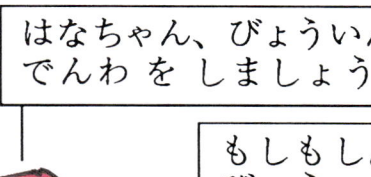

いいましょう 一

① きょうしつ

② みせ

③ こうてい

④ へや

⑤ たいいくかん

Using the examples as a guide, talk about where りえさん is.

例:
A りえさんは どこに いますか。
B きょうしつに います。

例:
A りえさんは どこですか。
B きょうしつです。

いいましょう 二

Using the example below as a guide, talk about where the animals are.

例:
A かめ は どこ に いますか。
B いす の うえ に います。

Using the example below as a guide, ask ひろしくん about his pets.

例:
A ペット を かって いますか。
B はい、ねこ を 三びき かって います。

いぬ を 一ぴき かって います。

いいましょう 三

㈠
コーヒー を のみます。

㈡
しんぶん を よみます。

㈢
しゅくだい を します。

㈣
ギター を ひきます。

㈤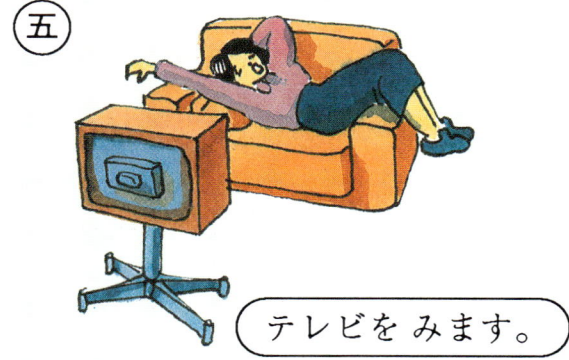
テレビ を みます。

㈥
てがみ を かきます。

Using the example as a guide, talk about these activities.

例:
A よく コーヒー を のみますか。
B いいえ、あまり のみません。

ともだちと

Make up a conversation with a partner.
Decide who will be A and who will be B.

A: [B]さんの かぞくは 何人 ですか。

B: | 四人 / 五人 / 六人 | です。父と母と | おとうと / あにが二人とあね / あねといもうと / あにとおとうと | が います。 |

A: そう ですか。ペットを かって いますか。

B: ええ、| いぬ / ねこ |を| 一ぴき / 二ひき / 三びき |かって います。

かぞくの しゃしんを みせましょうか。

A: ええ、みせて ください。この 人は だれ？

B: | あね / あに / いもうと / おとうと |です。| しょうがく 二ねんせい / ちゅうがく 一ねんせい / こうこう 三ねんせい |です。

A: そう ですか。| せが たかい / めが おおきい / きれい / ハンサム |ですね。| マスクを して いますね。 / スキーを して いますね。 / じょうばを して いますね。 / えを かいて いますね。 |

B: ええ、| スポーツが すき です。 / どうぶつが すき です。 / えが じょうず です。 / せんしゅう かぜを ひいて いました。 |

A: へえ... この 人は お父さん ですね。

B: はい、父は いま | イギリス / アメリカ / ヨーロッパ / 日本 | に います。

A: あ、そう ですか。

いってみましょう

― ごかぞくは何人ですか。

一

かぞくは 四人 です。父 と 母 と あねが います。あねの なまえ は ひろこです。

二

ぼくの かぞくは 三人 です。父 と 母 と ぼく です。ぼく は 二さい です。

三

かぞくは 四人 です。父 と 母 と いもうとが います。いもうとの りえこ は 六さい です。いぬ を 一ぴき かって います。

四

かぞくは 五人 です。父 と おじいちゃん と おばあちゃん が います。そして ひいおばあちゃん も います。ひいおばあちゃん は 八十二さい です。

ひいおばあちゃん　great grandmother

These people have told you about their families. Ask your friend about his or her family. You might ask questions such as:

・ごかぞく は 何人 ですか。
・おにいさん は 何さいですか。
・いもうとさん は 何ねんせい ですか。
・ペット を かって いますか。

二　Market research

Your class has been commissioned by a leading Japanese pet food manufacturer to find out which is the most popular pet food.
In groups of 5 or 6, find out:

・who has pets and what they are
・which brand of food each pet eats

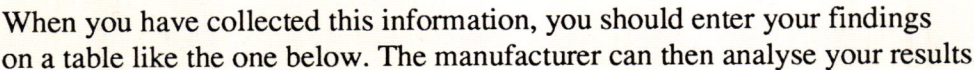

When you have collected this information, you should enter your findings on a table like the one below. The manufacturer can then analyse your results.

なまえ	ペット	ペット フード
ピーター	いぬ	Frend
サリー	ねこ	Purr
マーク	いぬ	Frend と Chew
	ねこ / 二ひき	Purr

日本語 ノート

一　Where are they?

The verb います means *be (in a place)*. When you use います to tell where people or animals are, you must put に after the place.

e.g. ケンくん は こうてい に います。
　　 Ken is in the school ground.

いません is the negative form of います.
You can use it to say that someone is not there.

e.g. たろうくん は へや に いますか。
　　 Is Taroo in his room?
　　 いいえ、いません。
　　 No, he's not.

If you want to give more detailed information about where people (or animals) are, you can use expressions like:

まりこさんは みせのまえ に います。
Mariko is in front of the shop.
へび は いすのした に います。
The snake is under the chair.

You can also use です instead of (に) います to find out where people or animals are.

e.g. アマンダさん は どこ ですか。
　　 Where's Amanda?
　　 としょかん です。
　　 She's in the library.

います cannot be used to tell where things are.

二　Talking about your family

います is also used when you are talking about your family and giving details. In this case います means *have*. You must put が after the person.

e.g. いもうと が います。
　　 I have a little sister.

If you have more than one sister, you must include the number using the counting system for people, 一人 (ひとり), 二人 (ふたり), 三人 (さんにん), 四人 (よにん) etc. To explain that you have two younger sisters, you would say いもうと が 二人 います.
The counter for people comes before the verb.

おとうとが一人います。

いぬを かって います。
I have a dog.
びょういん は こんで います。
The hospital is crowded.

はらじゅく は こんで いますね。

三　Talking about your pets

When you want to say how many pets you have, you must use the -ひき, -びき, -ぴき counter for animals. This counter comes before the verb.

e.g. いぬ を 三びき かって います。
　　 I have three dogs.

(If you do not have any pets, you can simply say ペット を かって いません。)

四　More about て います

In Unit 2, you learnt that a verb in て form followed by います tells us what someone is doing now. However, sometimes て います is used for an action or a state over a longer period. Look at these て います forms:

　おなか が すいて います。
　I am hungry.
　かぜ を ひいて います。
　I've got a cold.
　よこはま に すんで います。
　I live in Yokohama.

Remember that when you say this て います form, you need not pronounce い.

五　Saying what you don't do

The -ません form of the verb tells what you don't do.

e.g. あした がっこう に いきません。
　　 I'm not going to school tomorrow.

六　ごかぞく

When you ask someone who is older, or unknown to you, about their family, it is more polite to say ごかぞく.

e.g. やまださん、ごかぞく は 何人 ですか。
　　 How many people in your family, Mr Yamada?

七　More about と

と is a useful word that means both *and* and *with*. Compare these two sentences:

　父 と 母 と あね が います。
　(In my family,) there's my dad, mum and my older sister.
　ともだち と さんぽ に いきました。
　I went for a walk with my friends.

せいかつ

Hi everyone,

Big news! I've just found out that I'm related to a superstar. Well, almost. It's Yoko Tanaka. You know, Tanaka, as in Mr and Mrs Tanaka, the people I'm staying with. Yoko is their cousin or their niece or something. Well, I'm pretty sure she is, anyway.

I suppose you haven't heard of her. You know how in my last letter I told you I went to see Madonna in concert, well, what I didn't tell you is that Japan has its own pop industry and people here probably buy more Japanese records than ones from America, England or Australia. I've included a cutting from a Japanese pop magazine to give you an idea of how everyone is into it over here and to prove what I'm saying about Yoko Tanaka is all true. Her name is written in ローマじ on the poster too. The かんじ for Tanaka Yoko is 田中陽子.

I actually met Yoko a couple of times and she just seemed like any other Japanese teenager to me. I didn't even know she was training to be a star. You see, what happens here is that you get selected at an audition by one of the big recording companies and they work really hard to make you into a star. They put you through this really intensive instruction program, including voice and dance lessons, aerobics, public relations, fashion — everything you need to know about how to be an アイドル かしゅ. If you don't make it through the program you just go back to school and go on with your work. If they decide to package you as a star, then you get a chance to really make it big. That's what has happened to Yoko. One day nobody has heard of her, the next day she is everywhere!

She has a regular spot on Japan Sunday Hit Paradise and she is going to be in this new soapie called Top Stewardess. There's even going to be a special animated program about Yoko on Tuesdays at six o'clock. You can buy Yoko posters and even Yoko telephone cards. And like all the new アイドル かしゅ — there are about 75 of them introduced each year — she has made an 'image video'. We had a look at Yoko's video last night. It made her out to be super-cute, innocent, lovable girl-next-door, with typical teenage problems. That's so we can all identify with her, I suppose. And with her debut single you get a personal profile that includes her name, age, birthplace, hobbies, and even her bloodgroup! The bloodgroup is supposed to tell you a lot about a person's character or personality.

If everything goes well for Yoko, if her career really takes off, she will become like a goddess, a role model for every teenage girl. They will hang on every word she says and imitate the way she dresses. But if people just don't buy the 'package', then Yoko will just go back to school and get on with ordinary life. A lot of these overnight sensations seem to come and go all the time. She should make sure she continues her studies anyway, because she'll be finished by the time she's about 19 or 20. All the アイドル かしゅ are. When they reach that age, they just farewell all the millions of adoring fans and get married and have children.

Actually, she will have quite a lot of competition. The かわいい idol singers aren't quite as popular as they used to be. Their place is being taken by singing groups and by bands. I've included a couple of fan cards to give you the idea. You can buy these photos everywhere.

This is Wink. Wink is really popular here at the moment. When they sing they do all these complicated hand movements in time together and of course all the fans imitate them. Everyone does it. It's funny to see a businessman in a suit in his car stopped at a traffic-light start to do these movements when a Wink song comes on the radio.

This card is of ひで, a member of X. I saw one of their concerts at the とうきょうドーム on TV. One thing I can say about their music is it was LOUD! You couldn't really hear what they were singing but everyone in the audience was getting up and dancing and clapping. That's what is called the スピード feeling and that's what the new bands try to give their audiences. A lot of the bands sing quite a lot of English words but the thing is, they don't mean anything. They really don't. Sometimes people at school ask me what the words mean, and when I can't make any sense of them they think it's because I don't know Japanese well enough to translate properly, and they go away really disappointed. I mean, what would you make of this? 'Positive dance, friend feel'. Now when anyone asks me I just make something up like 'I really love you baby' and everyone is happy.

Even though they are getting away a little bit from the かわいい image for their stars, the bands just can't bring themselves to be anti-fashionable. There is a new all-female band called Princess Princess and they have a really great sound, I think. But everyone I hear talking about them discusses what they wear and how they want to get way-out dresses just like them. I sometimes think they are just as much fashion models as singers.

Anyway, we're all hoping that Yoko Tanaka can stay on top for a few years. If she doesn't, it won't be the fault of her managers at the record company. They have proclaimed every 8th day of the month 'Yoko Day'. I'll be doing my bit to help her. I'll be in my Yoko Tanaka T・シャツ with my Yoko Tanaka badge, have my B2-size poster on my wall and buy all the products that she advertises in the TV commercials.

Anyway, must dash — Top Stewardess is coming on TV. If I miss it, I won't know what everyone is talking about at school tomorrow.

Lots of love,
Simone シモーン

P.S. Don't forget, 'Positive dance, friend feel'.

単語

1	いっぴき	一ぴき	
2	にひき	二ひき	
3	さんびき	三びき	
4	よんひき	四ひき	
5	ごひき	五ひき	
6	ろっぴき	六ぴき	
7	ななひき	七ひき	
8	はっぴき	八ぴき	
9	きゅうひき	九ひき	
10	じゅっぴき	十ぴき	

1	ひとり	一人	
2	ふたり	二人	
3	さんにん	三人	
4	よにん	四人	
5	ごにん	五人	
6	ろくにん	六人	
7	しちにん	七人	
8	はちにん	八人	
9	きゅうにん	九人	
10	じゅうにん	十人	

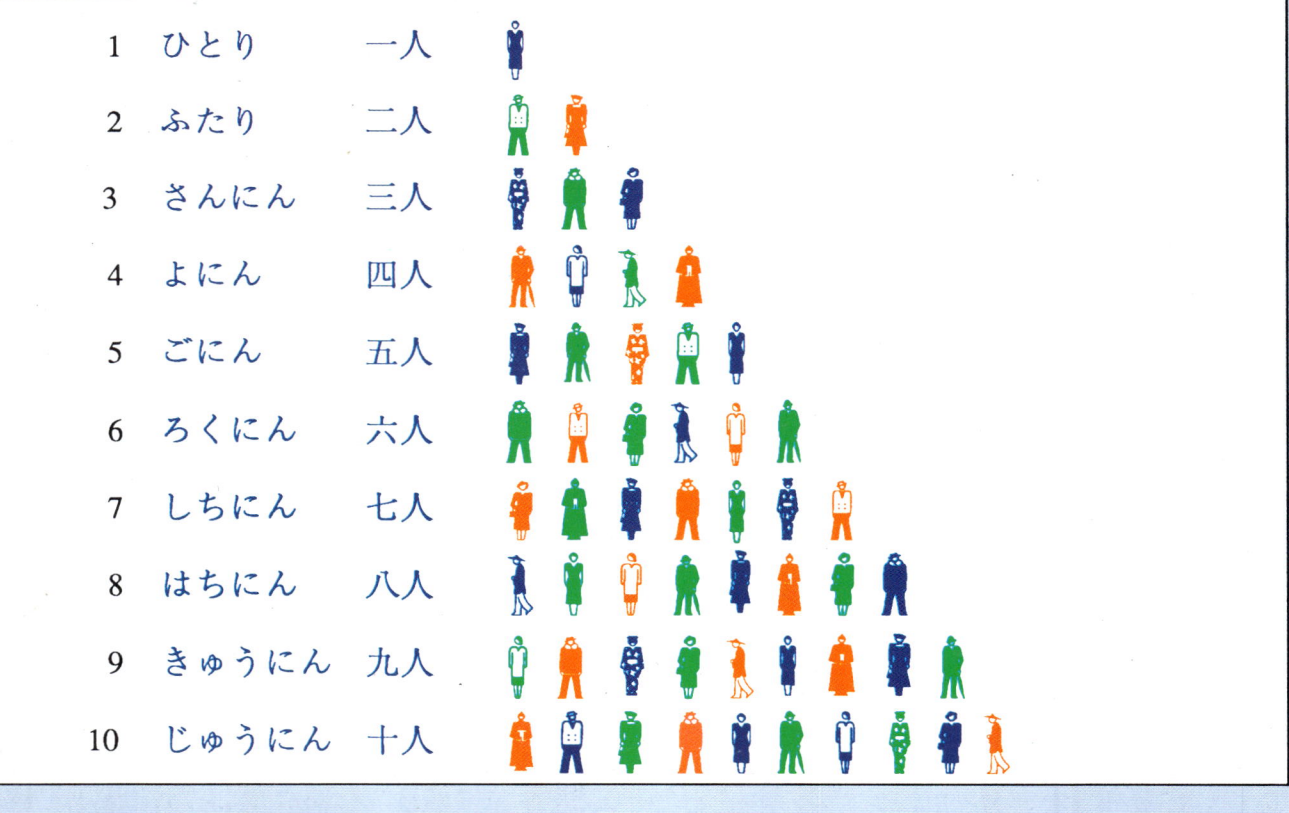

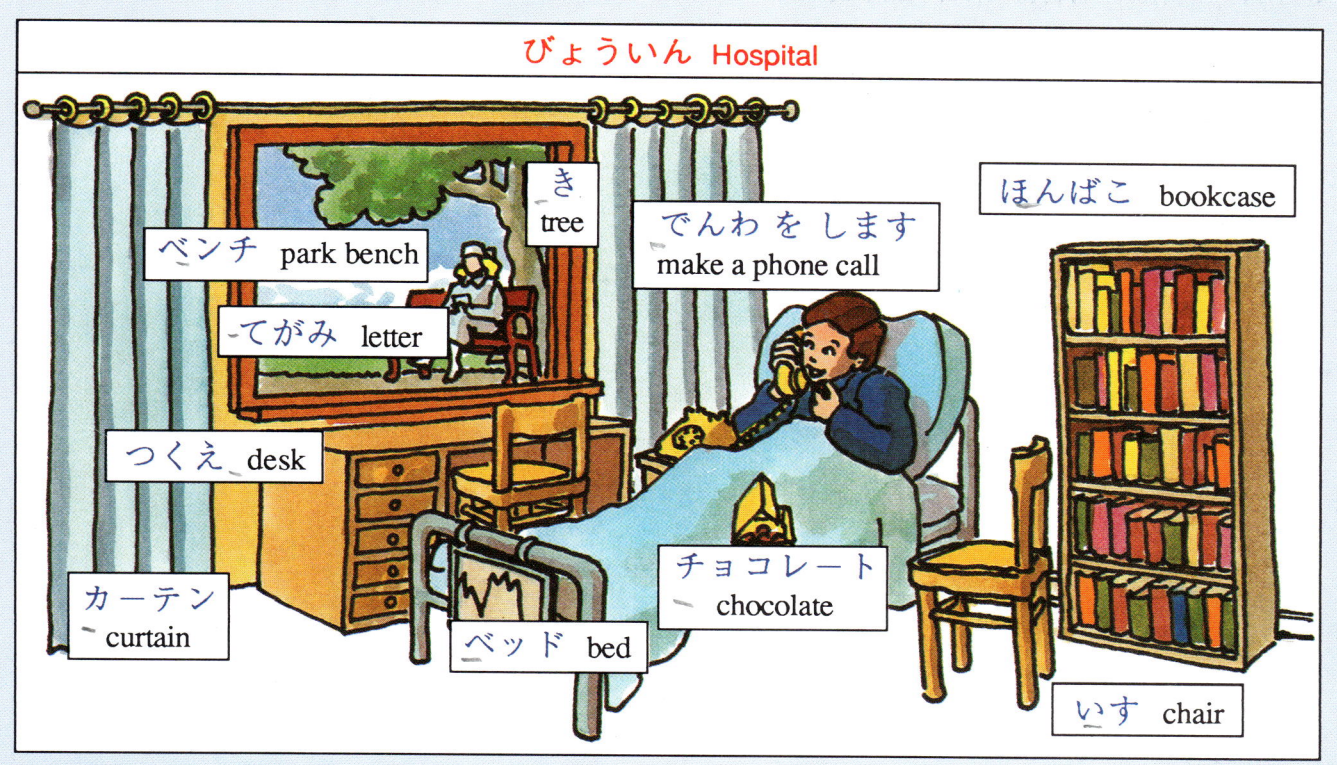

びょういん Hospital

- ほんばこ — bookcase
- き — tree
- でんわ を します — make a phone call
- ベンチ — park bench
- てがみ — letter
- つくえ — desk
- カーテン — curtain
- ベッド — bed
- チョコレート — chocolate
- いす — chair

どうぶつ Animals
- かめ — tortoise
- さかな — fish
- ぶた — pig

Locations
- うえ — on, above, up
- うしろ — behind
- した — under, below, down
- まえ — in front of
- きょうしつ — classroom

Expressions
- おなか が すいて いますか。 — are you hungry?
- こら! — you're in big trouble!
- こんで います — it's crowded
- たくさん — lots, many
- なまけもの — lazy, lazy thing
- はずかしかった — how embarrassing
- ふとりすぎ — he's too fat
- わたし じゃない — not me

おめでとう!

You are now able to use your 日本語 to:

- ask and tell where people and animals are
- give information about your family
- ask someone about their family and pets
- talk about your pets
- count people and animals
- talk about things that you don't do much

いいましょう 一

Using the example as a guide, talk about what time おさむくん got up during last week.

例:
> A きんようび に 何じ に おきましたか。
> B 六じ 四十五ふん に おきました。

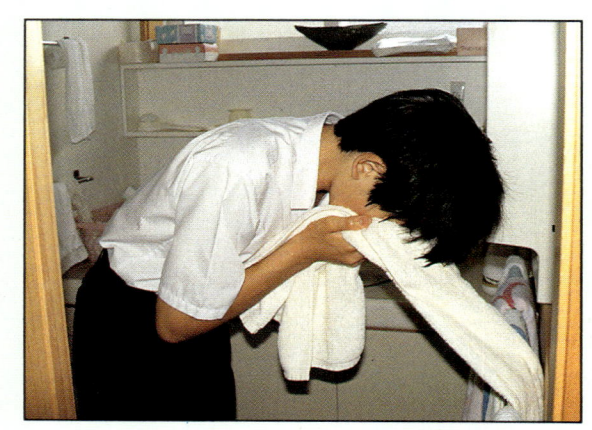

いいましょう 二

  10 キロ 300 メートル

  100 メートル 2 キロ

   100 メートル 1 キロ

  50 メートル 25 メートル

  3 キロ 200 メートル

Using the example as a guide, talk about each character's training program.

例:

A マイクくん、どんな トレーニング を しますか。
B 10キロ はしって、三びゃく メートル およぎます。それから エアロビクス を します。

いいましょう 三

ようふく

ポロシャツ

トレーナー
トレパン
スニーカー

パーカ
ジャケット
ジーンズ

パジャマ

スカーフ
セーター
スカート

Using the example as a guide, discuss the clothes in the catalogue.

例:

> A すてきな ポロシャツ ですね。
> B ええ、[A]さん は ときどき ポロシャツ を きますか。
> A ええ、よく きます。
>   or
> A いいえ、ぜんぜん きません。
>   あまり

> A すてきな ジーンズ ですね。
> B ええ、[A]さん は ときどき ジーンズ を はきますか。
> A ええ、よく はきます。
>   or
> A いいえ、ぜんぜん はきません。
>   あまり

きせつ

はなこさん and ゆうこさん are giving a talk about the seasons in Japan.

はる spring
三月 March
四月 April
五月 May

あき autumn
九月 September
十月 October
十一月 November

ふゆ winter
十二月 December
一月 January
二月 February

なつ summer
六月 June
(つゆ rainy season)
七月 July
八月 August

あき
あき は すずしい です。九月 に ときどき たいふう が きます。十一月 に やま で こうよう を 見ます。とても きれい です。

ふゆ
ふゆ は さむい です。たまに とうきょう で ゆき が ふります。ほっかいどう では ゆき が たくさん ふります。よく やま に 行って、スキー を します。

なつ
日本 の なつ は あつい です。六月 は つゆ です。まいにち あめ が ふります。いやですよ。七月 と 八月 は なつ やすみ です。よく うみ で すいえい を します。そして やま に ハイキング に 行きます。

はる
はる は あたたかい です。四月 に はなみ を します。きのした に すわって、ピクニック を します。はなみ の おべんとう は おいしい です。たのしい ですよ。

すずしい ___ cool	さむい ___ cold
たいふう ___ typhoon	ゆき が ふります ___ it snows
こうよう ___ autumn colours	あたたかい ___ warm
つゆ ___ rainy season	はなみ ___ flower viewing
あめ が ふります ___ it rains	おべんとう ___ a boxed lunch

ともだちと

Make up a conversation with a partner. Decide who will be A and who will be B.

こうていで　A | [B]さん、/[B]くん、 | どうしたんですか。

B | のど/あし/おなか | がいたいんです。/いまかぜをひいています。/きのうからてをしました。/きのうチョコレートをたくさんたべました。

A | そうですか。じゃ | うちにかえりますか。/びょういんに行きますか。

B | いいえ、 | サッカー/バスケット/けんどう/すいえい | のトレーニングに行きます。

らいしゅうクラブのキャンプに行きます。

A | いいですね。

B | よくないですよ。まいにちあさの五じ十ぷんにおきて | トレーニングをします。/十キロはしります。/プールでおよぎます。

A | へええ？

B | [A]さん、/[A]くん、 | すてきな/いい | テニスシューズ/バスケットシューズ/パーカ/スポーツシャツ | をはいていますね。/をきていますね。

[A]さん/[A]くん | はどんなスポーツをしますか。

A | スポーツは | すきじゃないです。/ぜんぜんしません。/あまりしません。 | でも、この | テニスシューズ/バスケットシューズ/パーカ/スポーツシャツ | は

かっこいいですね。

せいかつ

> がくねん(学年)　School year

```
       四月
日 月 火 水 木 金 土
       1  2  3  4  5  6
 7  8  9 10 11 12 13
14 15 16 17 18 19 20
21 22 23 24 25 26 27
28 29 30
```

> 四月に にゅうがく しき(入学式)が あります。
> 一ねんせいは あたらしい せいふくを きて、がっこうに きます。

> にゅうがく しき　new student entrance ceremony
> あります　there is

```
       五月
日 月 火 水 木 金 土
             1  2  3  4
 5  6  7  8  9 10 11
12 13 14 15 16 17 18
19 20 21 22 23 24 25
26 27 28 29 30 31
```

> 五月に しけんが あります。せいとは がんばって、べんきょう します。

> 三ねんせいは しゅうがく りょこう(修学旅行)に 行きます。

> しけん　exams
> しゅうがく りょこう　school trip

```
       六月
日 月 火 水 木 金 土
30                    1
 2  3  4  5  6  7  8
 9 10 11 12 13 14 15
16 17 18 19 20 21 22
23 24 25 26 27 28 29
```

> 六月は つゆです。まいにち あめが ふります。

```
       七月
日 月 火 水 木 金 土
       1  2  3  4  5  6
 7  8  9 10 11 12 13
14 15 16 17 18 19 20
21 22 23 24 25 26 27
28 29 30 31
```

> インターハイの きせつです。

第五課　七十

八月						
日	月	火	水	木	金	土
					1	2	3
4	5	6	7	8	9	10
11	12	13	14	15	16	17
18	19	20	21	22	23	24
25	26	27	28	29	30	31

なつやすみ です。クラブの れんしゅう と キャンプ を します。

れんしゅう practice
はじまります begin

九月						
日	月	火	水	木	金	土
1	2	3	4	5	6	7
8	9	10	11	12	13	14
15	16	17	18	19	20	21
22	23	24	25	26	27	28
29	30					

がっこう は はじまります。

十月						
日	月	火	水	木	金	土
		1	2	3	4	5
6	7	8	9	10	11	12
13	14	15	16	17	18	19
20	21	22	23	24	25	26
27	28	29	30	31		

しけんが あります。そして スポーツ ディ も あります。がんばれ！

十一月						
日	月	火	水	木	金	土
					1	2	3
4	5	6	7	8	9	10
11	12	13	14	15	16	17
18	19	20	21	22	23	24
25	26	27	28	29	30	

ぶんかさい(文化祭)か コンサート が あります。たのしい ですよ。

ぶんかさい cultural festival

十二月						
日	月	火	水	木	金	土
30	31					1
2	3	4	5	6	7	8
9	10	11	12	13	14	15
16	17	18	19	20	21	22
23	24	25	26	27	28	29

ふゆやすみ に クリスマス と おしょうがつ が あります。ときどき スキー に 行きます。

一月						
日	月	火	水	木	金	土
		1	2	3	4	5
6	7	8	9	10	11	12
13	14	15	16	17	18	19
20	21	22	23	24	25	26
27	28	29	30	31		

三ねんせい の しけんが あります。

おしょうがつ New Year

二月						
日	月	火	水	木	金	土
					1	2
3	4	5	6	7	8	9
10	11	12	13	14	15	16
17	18	19	20	21	22	23
24	25	26	27	28		

三月 に そつぎょうしき (卒業式) が あります。はるやすみ は はじまります。

そつぎょうしき graduation ceremony

がんばれ

Active listening

The first thing that strikes you when you hear two Japanese people conversing is that the listener seems to have nearly as much to say as the speaker. A Japanese listener always takes an active part in a conversation, chiming in with ああ、そう and そう ですか. These are just two of the 'response expressions' that are used in Japanese to show interest in what is being said and to encourage the speaker to go on. Do we have anything like this in English?

This practice is even more noticeable during telephone conversations in Japanese. Since the listener can't be seen, he or she works overtime on the 'response expressions' and may show agreement by saying そう そう そう! If the speaker feels a lack of this sort of listener feedback, he or she will check that the other person is still on the line with an urgent cry of もしもし. Does anything like this happen during English telephone conversations?

Take every opportunity to use these response expressions, especially during いってみましょう activities. They offer you a fun way of sounding genuinely Japanese. But don't forget to pay attention to intonation, i.e. the tone of voice that you use. For example, そう ですか can mean that you are really interested or that you doubt the truth of what is being said. It all depends on how you say it. Here are some other, similar expressions that you know.

そう ですね	to show that you agree, or that at least you're thinking about it
へえ?	to show that you are surprised or impressed
ほんとう?	to show that you doubt the truth of what is being said or that you are surprised

So, don't forget: even when your main job is to listen, you still have to hold up your end of a Japanese conversation.

いってみましょう

へえ?

Make up ten sentences describing things that you do. These could include your morning routine, or your weekend activities. Try to include the times when you do these things. Don't feel tied down by the truth — let your imagination run free! Your friend will respond to your statements using some response expressions. He or she might use those below.

いい ですね。	That sounds good!
はやい ですね。	That's early!
わたしも、ぼくも。	Me too.
うそ です。	That's a lie! I don't believe you!
ほんとう?	Really?
そう ですか。	Yeah?

まいあさ 五じに おきますよ。 / へえ? ほんとう?

Have your partner tell you his or her statements and respond appropriately.

日本語 ノート

一 Telling the time

You already know how to tell the time on the hour and half-hour. To tell the time in intervals of 5 minutes, you use 五ふん (ごふん), which means five minutes.

Look at these examples.

> いま 六じ 五ふん ですね。
> It's now 6.05.
> 七じ 十五ふん に あいましょう。
> Let's meet at 7.15.

十ぷん (じゅっぷん) means ten minutes and you can use this to tell the time in 10-minute intervals.

> いま 九じ 十ぷん ですね。
> It's now 9.10.
> 十じ 四十ぷん に 行きましょう。
> Let's go at 10.40.

When you want to meet your friend at 7.50, you can say,

> 七じ 五十ぷん に あいましょう。
> Let's meet at 7.50.
> or
> 八じ 十ぷん まえ に あいましょう。
> Let's meet at 10 to 8.

まえ means *in front of* or *before*. If you are doing something at a particular time, don't forget to use に after the time.

二 Getting dressed

There are several verbs that are used in 日本語 to talk about what you are wearing. The two most common ones are きます and はきます. When you wear items that you put your arms through, きます is used.

> e.g. おもしろい T・シャツ を きて いますね。
> You're wearing an interesting T-shirt.

Anything that you wear on the lower part of your body uses はきます.

> e.g. あたらしい くつ を はいて います。
> I'm wearing new shoes.

きます is used for clothing like a suit, a uniform or pyjamas. します can be used for a tie, belt or jewellery.

> e.g. ときどき イヤリング を します。
> I sometimes wear earrings.

三 More about the て form

To talk about a series of actions, you can use the て form of the verb. In this case, the て form has the meaning of the verb plus *and*.

> e.g. きのう まち へ 行って、おもしろい えいが を 見ました。
> Yesterday I went to town and saw a great film.
> まいあさ シャワー を あびて、せいふく を きて、がっこう に 行きます。
> Every morning I have a shower, put on my uniform and go to school.

The word それから, which means *after that* and そして, which means *and then*, are also useful for talking about the order of events.

四 あまり、ぜんぜん

When you want to say that you don't do something very often or you never do it, you use あまり and ぜんぜん with the verb in the negative -ません form.

> e.g. よく テニス を しますか。
> Do you play tennis often?
> いいえ、あまり しません。
> No, not very often.
> いいえ、ぜんぜん しません。
> No, never.

あまり is another way of saying あんまり. When you answer a question like おすし は すき ですか with いいえ、あんまり... you are shortening the statement いいえ、あんまり すき じゃない です。

単語

Time じかん

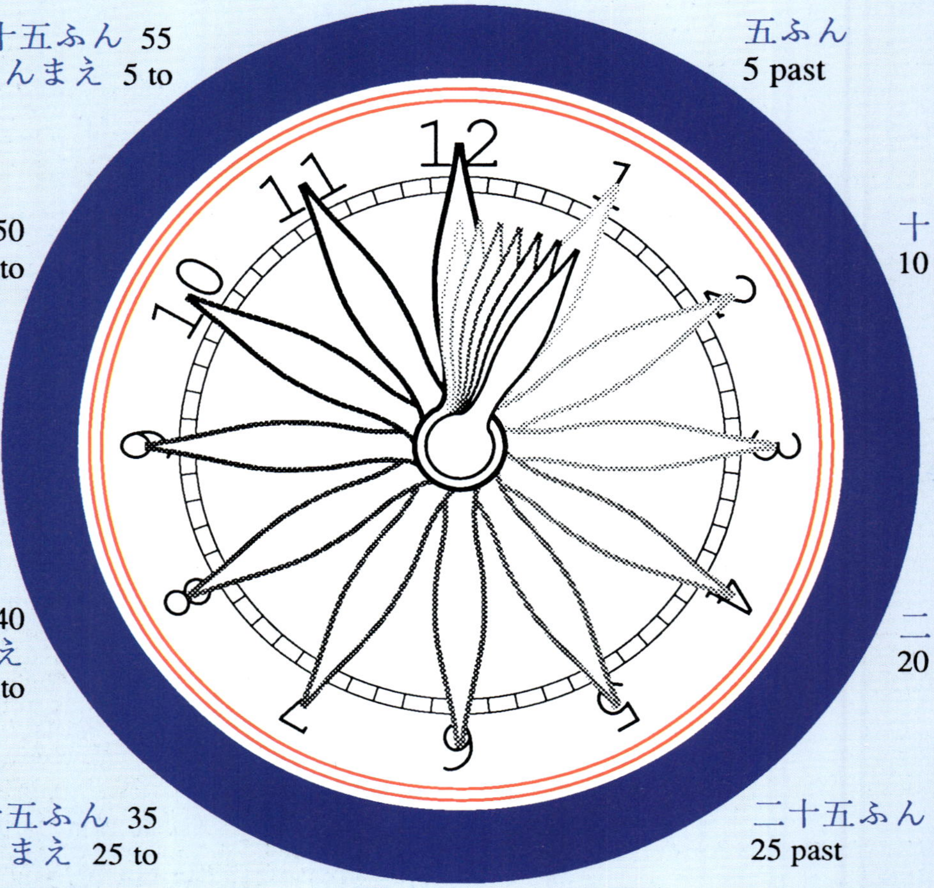

五十五ふん 55
五ふんまえ 5 to

五十ぷん 50
十ぷんまえ 10 to

四十五ふん 45
十五ふんまえ quarter to

四十ぷん 40
二十ぷんまえ 20 to

三十五ふん 35
二十五ふんまえ 25 to

三十ぷん 30
はん half past

五ふん 5 past

十ぷん 10 past

十五ふん quarter past

二十ぷん 20 past

二十五ふん 25 past

いま 何じ ですか。

New words

あまり	—	not often
いつも	—	always
ぜんぜん	—	never
たまに	—	occasionally
ときどき	—	sometimes
まい...	—	every...
まいにち	—	every day
よく	—	often
あさ	—	morning
あさごはん	—	breakfast
せいふく	—	school uniform
そして	—	and then
どんな	—	what kind of?

カタカナの 単語

アイスクリーム	—	ice-cream
オレンジ ジュース	—	orange juice
キロ(メートル)	—	kilo(metre)
コーンフレーク	—	cornflakes
トライアスロン	—	triathlon
トレーニング	—	training
ドーナツ	—	doughnut
ホット ドッグ	—	hot dog
ミートパイ	—	meat pie

Verbs

WEAK

(シャワー を) あびます	—	take (a shower)
おきます	—	wake up, get up
きます	—	put on, wear (top part of body)

STRONG

はしります	—	run
およぎます	—	swim
はきます	—	put on, wear (lower part of body)

Numbers 100 — 1,000

百	—	100	—	ひゃく
二百	—	200	—	にひゃく
三百	—	300	—	さんびゃく
四百	—	400	—	よんひゃく
五百	—	500	—	ごひゃく
六百	—	600	—	ろっぴゃく
七百	—	700	—	ななひゃく
八百	—	800	—	はっぴゃく
九百	—	900	—	きゅうひゃく
		1000	—	せん

いかが ですか。
How about this?

おめでとう!

You are now able to use your 日本語 to:

- talk about what you wear and don't wear
- talk about your morning routine
- tell someone what time it is (in 5- and 10-minute intervals)
- count to 1000
- talk about how often you do things

第六課 ベビー シッター は らくだなあ！

いいましょう 一

 一
 二
 三
 四
 五
 六

Using the example as a guide, ask permission to do or make use of various things.

例：

> A ファミコン を つかっても いい ですか。
> B ええ、いい です。（どうぞ）
>   or
>   いいえ、だめ です。

Using the example as a guide, give permission to do or make use of various things.

例：

> ファミコン を つかっても いい です。

Using the example as a guide, talk about how often you do or make use of various things.

例：

> A よく ファミコン を つかい ますか。
> B ええ、よく つかい ます。（だい すき です）
>   or
>   いいえ、ぜんぜん つかい ません。（きらい です）

These verbs might be of use
つかいます　のみます
つくります　はきます
見ます　　　食べます

いいましょう 二

Using the example as a guide, tell these children that they are not allowed to do these things.

例:
ピアノを ひいては だめ です。

Using the example as a guide, comment on the behaviour of these children.

例:
A あのこは ピアノを ひいて います。
B ひどい ですね。ピアノを ひいては だめ です。

This is a sign from an art classroom. What do you think is だめ in this room?

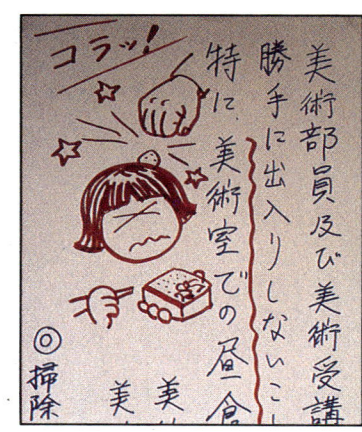

いいましょう 三

Tシャツ / ジャケット / パンツ

ブラウス / キャミソール / スカート

レインコート

Using the example as a guide, talk about the colour of these clothes.

例:
> A このジャケット は何いろ ですか。
> B あかい です。

Using the example as a guide, talk about whether you like these clothes.

例:
> A あかい ジャケット はすき ですか。
> B ええ、すき です。
> or
> いいえ、すき じゃない です。
> or
> いいえ、きらい です。

Using the example as a guide, talk about the colour of the advertised items.

例:
```
A このいろはすきですか。
B ブラックですか。
  はい、すきです。
  or
  いいえ、すきじゃないです。
```

東京 ディズニーランド の アンケート

This アンケート was compiled from the responses of students visiting 東京 ディズニーランド.

Q ディズニーランド へ 何かい 行きましたか。

A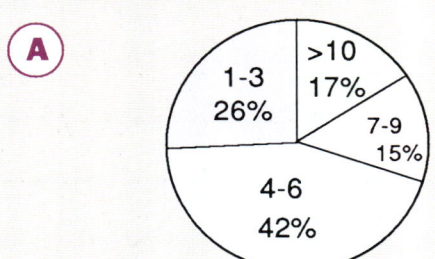
- 1-3 26%
- >10 17%
- 7-9 15%
- 4-6 42%

Q だれ と 行きましたか。

A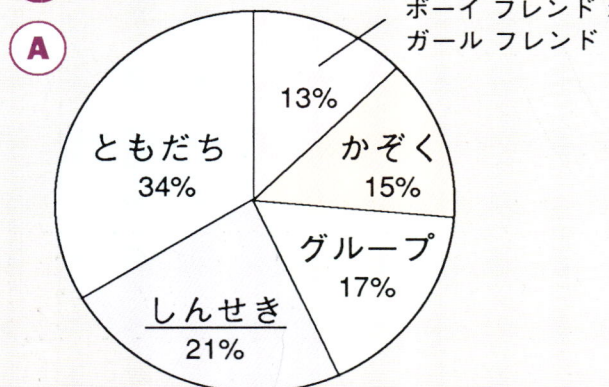
- ボーイ フレンド か ガール フレンド 13%
- ともだち 34%
- かぞく 15%
- グループ 17%
- しんせき 21%

Q すき な アトラクション は 何 ですか。

A
1. スペース・マウンテン
2. ビッグサンダー・マウンテン

Q スナック は 何 を 食べましたか。

A
1. ポップコーン
2. アイスクリーム
3. クレープ

Q パレード を 見ましたか。

A はい　95%
　　いいえ　5%

Q おみやげ は 何 を かいましたか。

A
1. ぬいぐるみ
2. キーホルダー
3. おかし

Q いくら つかいましたか。

A
1. 10,000－15,000円　49%
2. 5,000－10,000円　40%
3. >15,000円　9%

パスポート が 4,000円, のこりの 5,000円－10,000円 が 食事代 と おみやげ代 に なります。

アンケート	survey
何かい	how many times?
しんせき	relatives
ぬいぐるみ	stuffed toys
いくら	how much?
円 (えん)	yen

ともだちと

Make up a conversation with a partner. Decide who will be A and who will be B.

A: お母さん、ただいま。

B: あ、[B]さん、/[B]くん、おかえりなさい。| やきゅうの トレーニング / えい語の テスト | は どうでしたか。

A: よかった / むずかしかった / すごかった | ですよ。お母さん、おなか が すいてます。

いま | ケーキ / サンドイッチ / ハンバーガー | を | 食べても いいですか。/ つくっても いいですか。

B: いいえ、だめ ですよ。| りんご / オレンジ | を 食べて、| シャワーを あびて ください。/ おふろに はいって ください。

こんばん | おばあさんの うちに 行きます。/ レストランで ばんごはんを 食べます。/ お父さんと でかけます。

A: ああ、そう ですか。じゃ | ぼく / わたし | の あたらしい | ジーンズ / T・シャツ / テニス シューズ | を | きても いいですか。/ はいても いいですか。

B: いいえ、だめ です。その | あかい / ピンクの / くろい | パンツ / シャツ / くつ | を | きて ください。/ はいて ください。

A: お母さん...あれは | すきじゃない / きらい | ですよ。

第六課　八十五

せいかつ

Hi everyone,

I told you it would happen. You know all that fuss they made about Yoko Tanaka's debut, well, she has almost disappeared from the scene. I guess they'll now have someone else starring on Top Stewardess and making a video and writing a book and selling heaps of records.

But that's not why I'm writing. Mr Tanaka has just got his mid-year bonus and he is letting us each choose a present. He's really nice, because he has included me as well. They really treat me like one of the family now.

I'm not exactly sure what the bonus is for, but Mr Tanaka explained that nearly all Japanese workers get a big part of their annual pay in one go. Actually, it happens twice a year, once at the start of summer and once just before Christmas. Everyone really looks forward to these bonus times and all the shops put out brochures full of ideas on how to spend all that money! I cut out a few bits from these brochures so you will know what I'm talking about in the rest of the letter.

Let's start with the youngest. Haruko has asked for a ROBO portable sing-along system. It's called a パーティカラオケ. The one she wants lets you be a からおけ singer and that's just what Haruko wants to be. She can't wait until she's old enough to go into a karaoke bar and show off her talent.

She just sings all the time now. It's all because cousin Yoko told her she was かわいい and that she had a nice voice. Anyway, in these bars the customers get up and sing along with recorded music. The good thing about ROBO is that you can press a button to get wild applause and people screaming 'Encore!' I wouldn't mind a go myself.

Toshio wants to get a ビデオウォークマン. He says it's just essential because there is nothing to look at when you are walking around or travelling in the train. He can just see himself riding along on his bike, watching one of his favourite videos. Could be interesting! He wants the one you can plug into the car stereo system.

ビデオウォークマン

I'm next. What I really want is a ラップトップワープロ. It would be just great to be able to carry it around anywhere and do assignments and that.

パーティカラオケ

パーティースイッチ
「アンコール」
「ファンファーレ」

スピードコントロール

エコー

ラップトップワープロ

I could even write these letters on the train on the way to school. But I don't think it would be fair to ask for that, so I'm going to go for a コピーペン. They're just amazing. You just run them over some lines in a book, say, and then it will copy them into your notebook. It should be great for taking study notes, and if I ever go into the spy business.

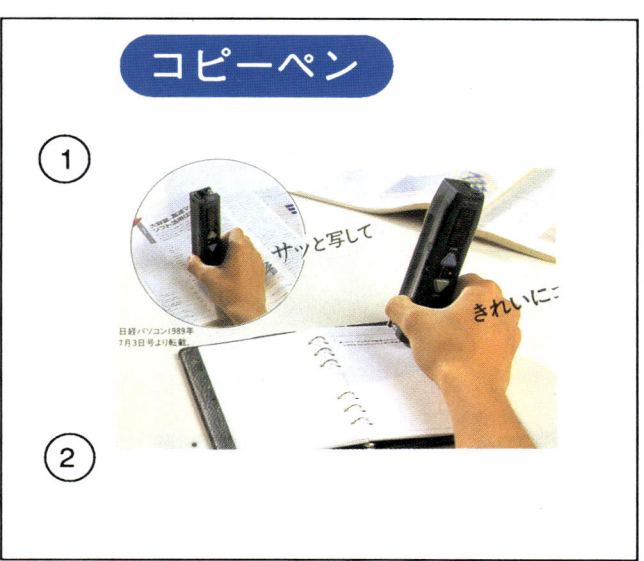

コピーペン

Mrs Tanaka is getting the most expensive thing. That's fair. It's a カラービデオプリンター. It works like this. Say you're watching a video and you see something you really like. Well, you freeze that frame, press a button and out comes a colour print of it. Amazing! Mrs Tanaka wants it so she can get prints from family videos, like Haruko's birthday party last week. I suppose they could use the fantastic camera they have, but it's not my business, really.

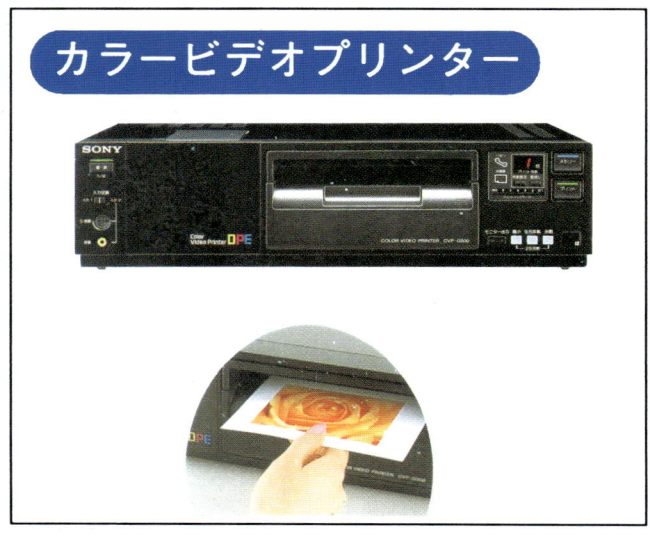

カラービデオプリンター

Poor Mr Tanaka is getting himself the most boring thing. It's called a パームトップコンピューター and as far as I can work out he can use it for business planning and records and communication and stuff like that. Anyway, I suppose he will have a go on the video printer when he feels like it.

パームトップコンピューター

Well, I hope I haven't bored you with all this. I just thought you'd like to see what's around over here. Sometimes I wonder about it all, but I suppose it all helps to make life better. I don't know. What do you think?

Anyway, must dash. I just heard Haruko scream and I think that means that Mr Tanaka is just arriving home. He just might have his arms full, so I might go and help him.

バイバイ
シモーン より

P.S. I'll post this tomorrow. Tonight I want to copy some of it into my diary. Guess what I'll be using to do it.

いってみましょう

1 でかけて も いい ですか。

You'd really like to go out with some friends, perhaps to see a film or have a pizza. You'll have to ask a parent permission for this and, of course, they will ask the usual questions, such as 'Where to? Who with? How will you get there? What time will you get home?' etc. etc...

Have your partner play the role of a concerned parent. If you can answer by making your parent feel confident that you are well organized, he or shewill let you go. This means that you will have to answer without too much hesitation!

2 でんわ を つかって も いい ですか。

Your parents are going overseas for six months and they are letting you choose a friend to live with.

Using a survey form like the one below, ask three friends if you'll be allowed to do these things at their place. Your friends should respond honestly, basing their answers on what they are permitted to do.

	ペニー	ロバート	ジョー
📺			
☎			
🍔			
🎸			
📼			
🎟			

Now that you have the answers, decide who you would prefer to move in with.

単語

何いろ　What colour?

あおい	blue
あかい	red
きいろい	yellow
くろい	black
しろい	white
ピンク(の)	pink
みどり(の)	green

Expressions

うん	yeah
きらい です	I hate it
して くれませんか	will you do this for me?
どうして？	why?
ドライヤ の なか	in the clothes-dryer
はやく	quickly, hurry up!
ひどい	dreadful, terrible, what a cheek!
もちろん	of course
らくだなあ	this is really easy, what a breeze!

New words

いっしょに	together
おふろ	bath
こどもたち	children
シャンプー	shampoo
ばんごはん	evening meal
ベビー シッター	baby-sitter
れいぞうこ	fridge
わたしたち	we

Verbs

でかけます	go out
ねます	go to bed, go to sleep
あります	there is, be (in a place)
つくります	make
とります	take
はいります	enter, go in
つかいます	use

おふろ に はいっています。

シャワー を あびています。

日本語 ノート

一 Asking permission

When you ask permission to do something, you add も いい ですか to the て form of the verb.

e.g. パーティー に 行って も いい ですか。
   May I go to the party?

If you are allowed to go, then your parent may say

ええ、いい です。
   Yes, that's OK.

If you are told, いいえ、だめ です, you are not allowed to go.

If you wish to tell someone that it is OK for them to do something, you can use this permission form without か.

e.g ジーンズ を はいて も いい です。
   It's OK to wear jeans.

二 Saying something is forbidden

When you want to say quite strongly that something is not allowed, は だめ です is added to the て form of the verb.

e.g. はしって は だめ です!
   No running!
   このみせ で 食べて は だめ です。
   You're not allowed to eat in this shop.

三 Love it or hate it?

In 日本語, as in English, there are many ways of saying how much you like or dislike something. Look at the list below:

だいすき	I really like it, I love it
すき	I like it
(あんまり) すき じゃない	I'm not that keen on it, I don't like it
きらい	I hate it
だい きらい	I can't stand it, I loathe it

People generally use (あんまり) すき じゃない when they don't like something, rather than the stronger words きらい and だいきらい.

四 何 いろ ですか。

Just when you thought you knew many colours in 日本語, you pick up a magazine or brochure and notice words like レッド and ブルー being used instead of あかい and あおい.

Just as in English when we use words like 'champagne' or 'milkwood' to describe beige and off-white, it is very popular in Japanese advertising to use the English colour words.

Colours that don't end in い are nouns in 日本語 and so の is used.

e.g. みどり の セーター を かいました。
   I bought a green jumper.

おめでとう!

You are now able to use your 日本語 to:

- ask if you may do something
- tell someone what they are allowed to do
- tell someone what they must not do
- talk about how much you like or dislike something
- describe something using a colour

第七課・この いす の あし は あります か。

いいましょう 一

Using the example as a guide, talk about the location of each shop.

例：

> A やおや は どこ に ありますか。
> B やおや ですか。やおや は にくや の となり に あります。
> or
> やおや は おかしや と にくや の あいだ に あります。

Using the example as a guide, talk about where things are.

例：

> A ポスト は どこ ですか。
> B パンや の まえ です。

Using the example as a guide, talk about your shopping.

例：

> A その バナナ を どこ で 買いましたか。
> B あの やおや で 買いました。

いいましょう 二

Using the example as a guide, do a stock-take in each section.

例：
> A 本は何さつありますか。
> B 六さつあります。
>
> A レタスはいくつありますか。
> B 四つあります。
>
> A マジックは何本ありますか。
> B 三本あります。

Using the example as a guide, find out if the item is in stock and buy it.

例：
> A はさみはありますか。
> B はい、あります。
> A じゃ、それをください。

Using the example as a guide, find out the price of the item.

例：
> A はさみはいくらですか。
> B 300円です。

Using the example as a guide, buy the items.

例：
> A りんごを五つください。
> B はい。
> じゃ、ぜんぶで500円です。

ともだちと

Make up a conversation with a partner. Decide who will be A and who will be B.

アイスクリーム の みせ で

A いらっしゃいませ。

B | チョコ チップ / パイナップル | の アイスクリーム は ありますか。

A すみません、きょう | チョコ チップ / パイナップル | は ありません。

B ああ、そう。じゃ、その | ピンク の / グリーン の / イエロー の | アイスクリーム は 何 ですか。

A これ ですか。これ は | ストロベリー / ペパーミント / バナナ | です。

B いくら ですか。

A シングル は | 150円 / 200円 | です。ダブル は | 200円 / 300円 | です。

B | シングル / ダブル | は | たかい / やすい | ですね。| ストロベリー / ペパーミント / バナナ | の | シングル / ダブル | を | 一つ / 二つ | ください。

A | 150円 / 200円 / 300円 / 400円 / 600円 | です。ありがとう ございます。

がんばれ

Accentuate the positive

Everyone learning Japanese, at one stage or another, gets a little bit discouraged by how hard it is to read the language. It can happen when a friend or family member asks you to read a brochure or a newspaper headline or sign, and you just can't do it.

But what these people may not realize is that for a Japanese learner, what comes first is speaking the language, a good practical skill that enables you to communicate with Japanese people. Whereas in, say, French or German, reading is perhaps the easiest language skill to acquire, in Japanese it is something requiring patient perseverance over a number of years. After all, it takes school students in Japan nine years to become familiar with all the characters in their own language!

This does not mean that you give up, of course. It just means that you have to be realistic and apply some positive reading skills to your Japanese reading. Let's take an example from the Disneyland survey in Unit 6.

パスポートが 4,000円、のこりの 5,000円 －10,000円 が 食事代 と おみやげ代 に なります。

You will notice that in this sentence we have highlighted everything you know. You can read 'passport' in katakana, you know the kanji for yen (円) and for food (食), and you surely recognise the word おみやげ. You also know that this question is about how money was spent by students at Disneyland.

This is what you need to do every time you attempt to read something in Japanese. Don't focus on what you don't know, but highlight what you do. You will still be left with some gaps in your understanding, but you can often fill some of these with some intelligent guessing at the meaning from the overall context of the sentence. In this way you can often come to understand the gist of what you are reading.

So, accentuate the positive: think about the rapid progress you have made in speaking Japanese and, when it comes to reading, concentrate on what you do know.

うた・かぞえましょう

ペット は どう かぞえるの?
いっぴき、にひき、さんびき、よんひきよ!
かぞえるのは やさしいよ!

ともだち は どう かぞえるの?
ひとり、ふたり、さんにん、よにんよ!
かぞえるのは やさしいよ!

じしょ は どう かぞえるの?
いっさつ、にさつ、さんさつ、よんさつよ!
かぞえるのは やさしいよ!

えんぴつ は どう かぞえるの?
いっぽん、にほん、さんぼん、よんほんよ!
かぞえるのは やさしいよ!

りんご は どう かぞえるの?
ひとつ、ふたつ、みっつ、よっつよ!
かぞえるのは やさしいよ!

いってみましょう

1 おみまい

You have probably heard how expensive some of the specially grown or imported fruit is in Japan. Below is a selection from a department store.

You and your friend are going to visit your teacher who is sick in hospital, and have decided to take some fruit. Take it in turns to point out what is available, how much it costs (whether or not it is expensive) and decide what you'll buy.

みかん
3kg 5,800円

オレンジ
20コ 3,500円

キーウィフルーツ
20コ 3,000円

さくらんぼ
1kg 6,000円

メロン
4,800円

パパイヤ
パパイヤ4コ、レモン1コ
3,500円

2 マクドナルド

You and your friend would both like to get a part-time job at マクドナルド on the ぎんざ during the summer holidays. You're both a bit worried about whether you'll be able to take down the orders and add up the prices quickly if the cash register breaks down.

Use the breakfast menu below to test each other. Take it in turns to decide what you'd like to have for breakfast and order it from your partner, who will take it down and tell you the total price.

You could take down the order in your own English (or Japanese!) shorthand, but you'll have to practise confirming the order and saying the prices in 日本語. Your order may sound like this:

ソーセージマフィン を 一つ、ハッシュポテト を 二つ ください。
そして ホット チョコレート を ください。

日本料理・Japanese food

If you visited Japan, you would find many familiar fast foods like スパゲッティ, ピザ and ハンバーガー, but why not try some *real* 日本料理.

すし is thin slices of raw fish resting on a small block of rice that has been flavoured with sweetened vinegar. This style of すし is called にぎりずし.

Beware of the わさび which is the very hot, green paste dabbed onto the rice. Can you guess why わさび has a nickname of なみだ (tears)?

Another popular style of すし is まきずし. This is strips of vegetables or fish placed on rice and rolled in のり seaweed. のり is dried seaweed which has been pressed into a crisp, flat, shiny sheet. The rolls are then cut into slices.

さしみ, like すし, is a raw fish dish. Slices of fresh fish are skilfully cut and arranged attractively. The slices are eaten after being dipped in soy sauce seasoned with わさび.

Another famous Japanese dish is てんぷら, which is a combination of pieces of fish and vegetables deep-fried in a very light batter. A dipping sauce with soy sauce, grated radish and ginger accompanies the dish. In some てんぷら restaurants in Japan, the てんぷら is cooked piece by piece in front of you and served to you immediately.

Accompanying these dishes and others may be soups such as みそしる or すいもの. みそしる is a soybean paste soup and many people enjoy it for breakfast. すいもの is a clear soup perhaps containing fish or chicken.

Of course Japan's staple food is rice (ごはん). The importance of rice is shown by the fact that the word ごはん means both *rice* and *a meal*. Steamed rice is served at nearly every meal. ごはん also is used as the base for a range of other dishes.

A quick lunch is てんどん which consists of deep-fried prawn cutlets on a bowlful of hot rice.

In Japan, the traditional 'fast food' has always been noodles. There are several kinds of noodles that are very popular. White うどん are made from wheat and are served piping hot in a soup, often with various accompaniments on top.

Brown そば noodles are made from buckwheat and these can also be served in a soup or they are tasty served with simply a dipping sauce.

Chinese noodles in 日本語 are called ラーメン and these are a popular dish to order in a Chinese restaurant or noodle shop.

All noodles are eaten with chopsticks and hearty slurping is not considered rude!

One-pot dishes cooked at the table are a regular family meal. The most famous of these is すきやき, a dish of thinly sliced meat, vegetables, とうふ (bean curd) and はるさめ (spring rain) noodles cooked together in a sweetened soy sauce broth.

Meals are completed with おちゃ, which is taken without milk or sugar.

日本語 ノート

一 Do you have...? Is there...?

In Unit 4 you learnt to use います to tell where people or animals are. To tell where things are, the verb あります is used. As with います, you must put に after the place.

e.g. パンや は あそこ に あります。
　　The bakery is over there.
　　うち は パンヤ の となり に あります。
　　Our house is next door to the bakery.

As with (に)います, です can be used instead of (に)あります.

e.g. でんわ は つくえ の うえ です。
　　The phone is on the desk.

あります is also used to mean *have*.

e.g. ピンク の マジック は ありますか。
　　Have you got a pink highlighter pen?
　　はい、あります。
　　Yes, I have.
　　いいえ、ありません。
　　No, I haven't.

二 In between

To say something is between two things, you must name the two things on either side and then add (の)あいだ.

e.g. うち は がっこう と こうえん の あいだ です。
　　Our house is in between the school and the park.

三 More about counting

You have learned to count your pets with the ひき counter for animals and to count friends and family with the り/にん (人) counter for people. There are many other counters used in 日本語. In some cases it depends on what is being counted. For example, if you want to count books, magazines etc., you must use さつ.

e.g. 本 を 三さつ 買いました。
　　I bought three books.

In other cases it depends on the shape of the item. When you are counting long, thin objects like pens, pencils, trees, bottles etc., the counter ほん (本) is used.

e.g. えんぴつ を 六本 買いました。
　　I bought six pencils.

Do note that you cannot count books (本) with the counter 本! さつ is counted in the same way as さい. To count one book is いっさつ, and eight books is はっさつ.

There is another number system that is used for things that do not clearly fit one of the 'counter' categories. These are the つ numbers.

e.g. ハンバーガー を 二つ 買いました。
　　I bought two hamburgers.
　　おかし を 八つ 食べました。
　　I ate eight sweets.

The つ numbers, which only go to ten, are widely used. Little children often use ひとつ (一つ), ふたつ (二つ), みっつ (三つ) to tell their age. *Ten* in the つ numbers is written とお(十). In many Japanese advertisements you will notice that こ(コ) is often used to count small objects like pieces of fruit, eggs etc. The counters and つ numbers go *before* the verb or ください.

四 Using ください

In きもの 1, you learned to ask people to do things using ください.

e.g. ペン を かして ください。
　　Please lend me your pen.

ください can also be used to ask for or to order things.

e.g. これ を ください。
　　Please give me this.
　　コーヒー を 二つ ください。
　　Two coffees, please.

五 ¥ = 円

Japanese currency is called えん. In かんじ it is 円 and ¥ is the international symbol. 円 goes after the number (百円) but ¥ goes before (¥100).

単語

New words

あいだ	between
うえき	pot plant
うります	sell
くま	bear
たんす	wardrobe
となり	next to
にく	meat
もの	things

Expressions

いくらですか	How much is...?
いらっしゃいませ	welcome, can I help you?
しんじられない	that's unbelievable
しょうがない	can't be helped
ぜんぶで (いくらですか)	(How much) in all?

Adjectives

すばらしい	wonderful
たかい	expensive, high
ふるい	old (for things)
りっぱ	great, magnificent
やすい	cheap

カタカナ の 単語

アンチック	antique
ガレージ セール	garage sale
ゴルフ クラブ	golf clubs
ゴルフ バッグ	golf bag
でんき スタンド	lamp
ポスト	post-box
マットレス	mattress
ランプ シェード	lampshade

本や bookshop

～さつ	counter for books
ざっし	magazine
じしょ	dictionary

ぶんぼうぐや stationery shop

はさみ	scissors
マジック	highlighter pen

やおや greengrocer

すいか	watermelon
みかん	mandarin
りんご	apple
やさい	vegetables

Numbers to 10 000

せん	1000
にせん	2000
さんぜん	3000
よんせん	4000
ごせん	5000
ろくせん	6000
ななせん	7000
はっせん	8000
きゅうせん	9000
いちまん	10 000

ココナツを ここのつ ください。

はい。

おめでとう！

You are now able to use your 日本語 to:

- ask and tell where something is
- ask what is available when shopping
- ask and tell how much things cost
- decide what to buy
- calculate the price of items
- count various objects
- count to 10 000

第八課・はし が つかえますか。

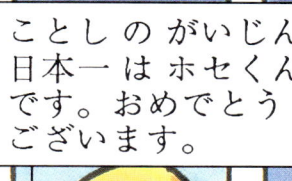

いいましょう 一

Using the example as a guide, talk about which script or language each character is using to write their essay.

例:

A ゆうこさん は ひらがな で かいて いますか。
B いいえ、カタカナ で かいて います。

いいましょう 二

Using the example as a guide, say which implement is best to use when eating these foods.

例:
> A てんぷら は て で 食べますか。
> B いいえ、はし で 食べます。

Using the example as a guide, talk about whether you are able to eat these foods.

例:
> A にく が 食べられますか。
> B はい、食べられます。
> or
> いいえ、食べられません。

いいましょう 三

Using the example as a guide, ask if someone is able to do these things or play these sports. The verbs in the box may be of use.

例:

A かんじ が よめますか。
B はい、すこし よめます。
or
いいえ、あまり よめません。

A テニス が できますか。
B はい、できます。
or
いいえ、できません。

よめます
できます
かけます
つかえます

ともだちと

Aさん は 日本人 です。Bさんは がいこく人 です。
でんしゃの なか で はなして います。

Make up a conversation with a partner. Decide who will be A and who will be B.

A: ここ に すわって もいい ですか。

B: はい、どうぞ。

A: あ、日本語 が はなせます / できます ね。

B: すこし はなせます。/ できます。 日本語 は おもしろい / むずかしい です。

A: ああ、そう ですか。ひらがな / カタカナ は どうですか。かけますか。/ よめますか。

B: はい かけます。/ よめます。 がっこう で べんきょう して います。

A: がっこう で...? どこから きましたか。

B: アメリカ / オーストラリア / ニュージーランド から きました。

A: ああ、そう ですか。せんせい は 日本人 / アメリカ人 / ニュージーランド人 / オーストラリア人 ですか。

B: はい、/ いいえ、 日本人 / アメリカ人 / ニュージーランド人 / オーストラリア人 です。 よく / いつも 日本語 / えい語 で はなします。

A: [B]さん / [B]くん は 日本語 が じょうず ですね。

B: いいえ、そう でも ない です。

せいかつ

Hi everyone,

We're just back from this really excellent holiday. I just have to write about it before I forget all the details. I'll put it all in this letter, then I'll copy the best bits into my diary with my コピー ペン.

Where do I start? Well, we went to 北海道 (ほっかいどう). I suppose you've forgotten where it is. Have you got a map or something? It's an island and it's a really brilliant place. It's just so different from the rest of Japan. You know how, when you think of Japan, you think of ancient temples and traditions and crowded cities nearly all joining up, well, in 北海道 it's just the opposite. It's like Japan's wilderness area, just so natural and sort of untouched. It's all volcanoes and forests and stuff like that.

We nearly didn't get to see all of this. Mrs Tanaka's idea was to go to さっぽろ, the modern capital of 北海道 and spend two weeks in a luxury hotel there. It's a really modern city with everything well planned and it's really easy to find your way around to all the shops. She told Mr Tanaka about the big brewery there and said that we could all go and watch them making beer. That would be fascinating!

You might have heard of さっぽろ. It's where they had the 1972 Winter Olympics. It's also where they have the Snow Festival in February. The locals make these fantastic sculptures in ice and snow. I don't just mean snowmen, I mean full-sized replicas of buildings like the Opera House or huge monsters or giant slides. Here's one of シャーロック ホームズ.

The main reason there aren't that many cities on 北海道 is that it has really only been settled since 1868. Well, there were native people living there. They are called ainu, and there are still some left, but not that many. We saw some of these Japanese aborigines in an ainu village. I suppose it was interesting, but I thought it was a bit sad because it was all touristy. They did this sort of native dance for us, but they didn't seem to have their hearts in it.

I haven't been there in winter, but I have seen it all on TV. In February, all the channels here have daily news broadcasts with the latest from the Snow Festival. About 2 million people go to the Snow Festival every year. I'm hoping to get there myself one year.

But I'm getting off the track, because we didn't really stay in さっぽろ and we didn't stay in a hotel, and we went in June. When we saw the holiday brochures about 北海道 and it being called キャンプロード, Toshio, Haruko and I wanted to go camping. It just seemed right to have a bit of a rugged holiday in this wild part of the world. The Tanakas didn't have any camping equipment, but you could hire everything you needed. I think it would have been really nice, with matching tent and camp furniture and sleeping bags and all that.

But Mrs Tanaka was not in the mood for roughing it, and besides all Mr Tanaka could talk about was which campervan (キャンピングカー) we would choose. He kept telling Mrs Tanaka how luxurious they were, and when he spoke to us he said it was just like camping — except that we would have more room for video walkmans and computers and other essentials. I have to admit the camper we chose was really nice and I got to have the bed over the driver's cabin.

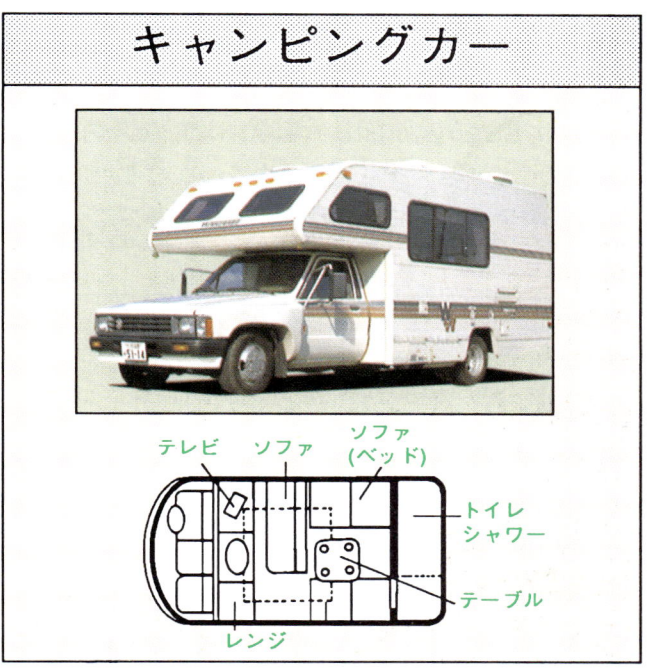

We didn't pick up our campervan until we got to 北海道. To get there, we took the しんかんせん to the north of ほんしゅう, then we caught another train which took us under the sea to 北海道 through the Seikan Tunnel. This tunnel is 53 kilometres long and we were all looking forward to going through it. It was a bit disappointing, really, because you were going along, and then it just became dark and that was it. Still, I don't know what I expected. Half-way through the tunnel we got out and visited the museum they have there that shows you all this stuff about how they built it and that. It was finished in 1988.

The best part of our holiday in 北海道 was just being in such a wild place. It wasn't all tame and civilised, if you know what I mean. Mr Tanaka had to drive the campervan really carefully because there were all these really steep cliffs and volcanic craters and we kept thinking about going over. The most famous 北海道 volcano just popped up in a potato patch in 1945 while the farmer was working in it. It grew 20 cm a day for seven months and it erupted. After the eruption 北海道 had a new volcano, nearly 400 metres high. Lots of the volcanic craters on the island are filled up with beautiful lakes and you can walk around them or hire boats to go cruising on them. Then there were also lots of hot springs and steaming mud pools all over the island — no wonder there are so many おんせん in 北海道. The most famous one is called のぼりべつ おんせん. It's a huge complex of all different types of hot spa baths, all with luxury hotels around. I wasn't interested in the おんせん, but I was really rapt in じごく だに. Know what that means? The Valley of Hell. When you see it, you know why. It's this huge crater full of boiling mud. It has this scary, hissing sound and the smell is just disgusting — just like rotten egg gas. They say it is a favourite place for suicides. What an off place to jump into!

Summer in and around とうきょう can be really hot and humid, so a lot of Japanese people come to 北海道 where it is a lot cooler and drier. We saw lots of other campervans, especially in だいせつざん National Park, right in the centre of the island. If you can't go anywhere else in 北海道, go there. You can see all forests and waterfalls and that, as well as bears and deer. Well, we saw some deer, but we didn't see any bears until we went to this bear ranch. It was all right, but the bears seemed really bored and lazy.

The best animals we saw were the foxes at the fox shrine which was right near a peppermint farm. That's right, peppermint. You see it growing everywhere in the cleared areas outside the National Park and the plants look really excellent when they are in flower. I didn't know peppermint came from a plant. I thought it was just a flavour. Anyway, these foxes were really cute and friendly. They're my favourite animal now, they're just so foxy.

I should mention some of the food we had, too. My favourite thing was いしかり なべ, which is a sort of soup made up of chunks of salmon with vegetables, seaweed and みそ bean paste. Salmon is one of the most popular foods in 北海道. In fact, they really go in for all sorts of fish and seafood. In one place we saw けがに. These are great hairy crabs. They had giant replicas of them hanging over the doorway of the restaurant. It is illegal to catch these crabs, but it's not illegal to eat them. We didn't try them, we had ジンギスカン instead. It's a sort of lamb stew. The thing is, you know that all the ingredients are fresh in 北海道 because that's where many of the farms and fisheries are.

Anyway, it was a really great holiday. It was a part of Japan I didn't really know anything about. The people were really great, too. Living up there they didn't seem to be so worried about traditions and customs. It's hard to explain, but they seemed a bit freer or something. We were glad to get home, but now the Tanakas are talking about going back in February for the Snow Festival. That would be really fantastic. Mrs Tanaka might get her stay in her posh hotel.

I hope you can read these bits of brochures I've sent with the letter. It doesn't matter if you can't understand them all — I can't either. But you should get a good idea about a lot of it.

I'll be home in a few weeks and I'm looking forward to catching up with you all again. Until then,

Lots of love,

シモーン　　　より

日本語 ノート

一　More about で

You have learned that で means *by* a mode of transport.

e.g. バス で かえりました。
　　 I came home by bus.

You have also used で to mean *at* (or *in*) a place.

e.g. みせ で 買いました。
　　 I bought it at the shop.

で can also be used to mean *in* a language, or *in* a script such as ひらがな or ローマじ.

e.g. あの人 は フランス語 で はなして います。
　　 He's speaking in French.
　　 じゅうしょ を ローマじ で かいて ください。
　　 Please write your address in romaji.

Yet another meaning of で is *with* an implement such as a pen or a knife.

e.g. はし で 食べました。
　　 We ate with chopsticks.
　　 えんぴつ で かいて は だめ です。
　　 Don't write in pencil.

二　Can you do this?

To ask if someone can do a certain thing or to tell what you are able to do, a change is made to the verb. Look at the list below.

はいります　→　はいれます
つかいます　→　つかえます
まちます　　→　まてます
かきます　　→　かけます
あそびます　→　あそべます
よみます　　→　よめます
はなします　→　はなせます

You have no doubt worked out that the い sound before ます is changing to an え sound, so り changes to れ, ち changes to て etc. The ひらがな chart also shows you what happens.

ま　み　む　め　も
ら　り　る　れ　ろ

Two groups of verbs are exceptions to this. One is the weak verb group.

食べます　→　食べられます
おきます　→　おきられます

e.g. にく が 食べられますか。
　　 Can you eat meat?

The other is the irregular verbs, where the verbs *do* or *play* and *come* change a lot.

きます　→　こられます
します　→　できます

e.g. あした こられますか。
　　 Can you come tomorrow?
　　 スポーツ が できますか。
　　 Can you play sport?

The final thing you have to remember when using this form is to put が after the thing you can do.

e.g. かんじ が よめます。
　　 I can read kanji.
　　 カタカナ が かけます。
　　 I can write katakana.

The question 日本語 が できますか is often asked of foreigners and while it means *Can you do Japanese?* it usually means *Can you speak Japanese?* You will, of course, be able to answer modestly はい、すこし できます.

三　Use of お

The sound お is often put in front of some words to give a more polite effect. This is done more frequently by female speakers. Many girls would say おはし for chopsticks. Boys could leave off the お in おはし in informal situations.

四　Use of へ

Like に, へ is also used to mean *to* a place. When it is used to mean *to* it is pronounced as *e*.

e.g. らいしゅう 日本 へ かえります。
　　 I'm returning to Japan next week.

いってみましょう

1 ホーム・ステー

としおくん is coming to stay with your family for a week on a home-stay program. The Japanese school organising the visit has sent the profile below.

Your mother is becoming a little anxious about the visit. Your partner will take the part of your mother and ask you lots of questions about としおくん.

For example, she wants to know if he is used to animals, if he plays any sports and if he is interested in music. She is also concerned about whether or not he is able to speak or read English, what he can eat and what he can use to eat with.

Using the profile below, reassure your mother about としおくん's visit.

なまえ： いけだ としお
ねんれい：14
かぞく： 4人 (父、母、あね)
ペット： ☑一ぴき ☑二ひき

おんがく：
- ☑すき ☐ひけます ☑ひけます
- ☐きらい ☑ひけません ☐ひけません

スポーツ：
- ☑できます ☑できます
- ☐できません ☐できません

- ☐できます ☑できます
- ☑できません ☐できません

えいご： よめます ☑よく　　はなせます ☐よく
　　　　　　　　 ☐すこし　　　　　　　　☑すこし

たべもの：きらいなもの: チーズ、トマト
　　　　　すき なもの: にく、スパゲッティー、フルーツ

ナイフ と フォーク ☑つかえます
　　　　　　　　　 ☐つかえません

2 ワープロ が つかえますか。

As supervisor of the zoo you have noticed that there are more and more Japanese bringing their children to see the animals. You've decided to hire someone to guide the children around and teach them about the animals in an entertaining way.

Certain skills are necessary for this special job. The person should like children and animals and be able to:

- speak Japanese
- write かんじ、ひらがな and カタカナ
- sing and play games
- use a word processor (for drawing up schedules etc.)
- come tomorrow

Draw up an interview sheet to record the details of each applicant (name, age, address, phone number) as well as their responses to your questions.

Interview three friends who will, of course, be very honest about their abilities, and decide who you will employ.

単語

New words	
がいこくじん (がいじん)	— foreigner
さくぶん	— essay
じゅぎょう	— lesson
だい	— title, topic
(お) はし	— chopsticks
ひるやすみ	— lunchtime

おめでとう

You are now able to use your 日本語 to:

- ask someone if they can do things
- tell someone what you can do
- explain what you use to eat with
- explain what language or script and what writing implement you use

Appendix
かんじ (漢字)

日

Meaning: *sun, day*

Readings
ひ (び)
にち (に)

日本 (にほん)
日よう日 (にちようび)

 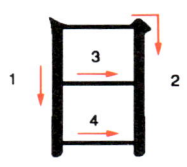

本

Meaning: *origin, book*

Readings
ほん (ぽん, ぽん)

日本 (にほん)
本 (ほん)

人

Meaning: *person*

Readings
ひと
じん、にん (り)

この人 (このひと)
日本人 (にほんじん)
三人 (さんにん)
二人 (ふたり)

語

Meaning: *language*

Readings
ご

日本語 (にほんご)
単語 (たんご)
フランス語 (フランスご)

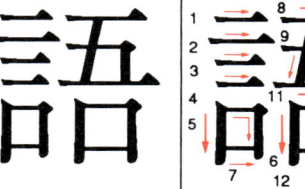

何

Meaning: *what?*

Readings
なに、なん

何語 (なにご)
何人 (なんにん)

 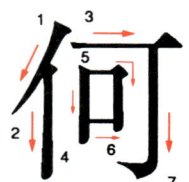

月

Meaning: *moon, month*

Readings
がつ、げつ

一月 (いちがつ)
四月 (しがつ)
今月 (こんげつ)
来月 (らいげつ)

母

Meaning: *mother*

Readings
はは
(お)かあ(さん)

母 (はは)
お母さん (おかあさん)

 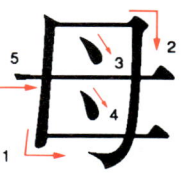

父

Meaning: *father*

Readings
ちち
(お)とう (さん)

父 (ちち)
お父さん (おとうさん)

行 行	見 見	食 食
Meaning: *go*	Meaning: *look, watch, see*	Meaning: *eat*
Readings い (きます)	Readings み (ます)	Readings た (べます)
行きます(いきます) 行って(いって)	見ます (みます) 見て (みて)	食べます (たべます) 食べて (たべて)
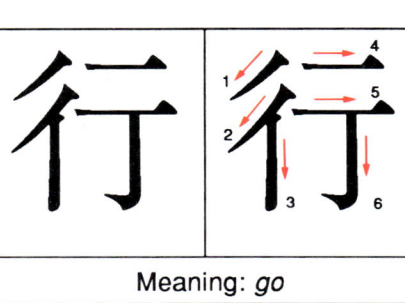	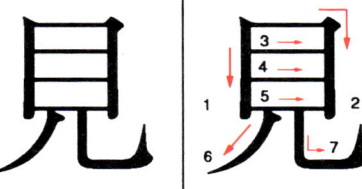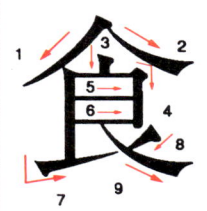	

買 買	円 円	山 山
Meaning: *buy*	Meaning: *yen*	Meaning: *mountain*
Readings か (います)	Readings えん	Readings やま
買います (かいます) 買って (かって)	百円 (ひゃく えん) 五円 (ごえん)	たかい 山 (たかい やま)
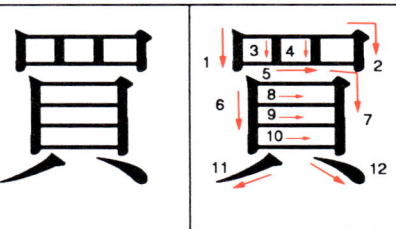	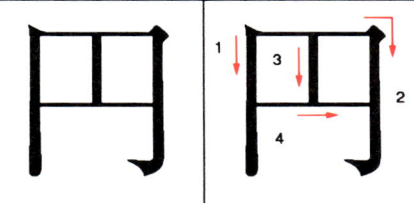	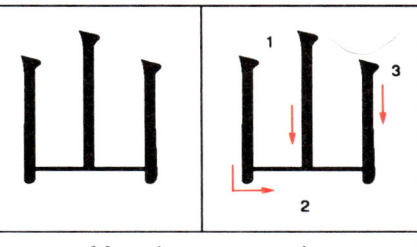

川 川	田 田	
Meaning: *river*	Meaning: *rice field*	
Readings かわ (がわ)	Readings た (だ)	
ながい 川 (ながい かわ) 山川さん (やまかわさん)	山田 さん (やまださん) 本田 さん (ほんだ さん)	
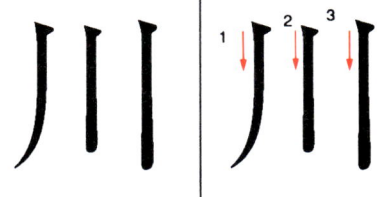	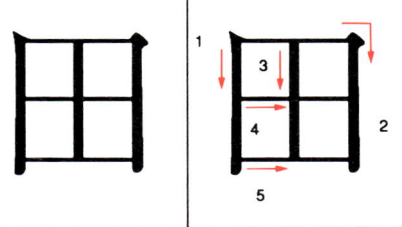	

漢字 ● 百十九

単語・日本語—英語

あ

アイス クリーム	ice-cream
あいだ	between
あおい	blue
あかい	red
あき	autumn
あさ	morning
あさごはん	breakfast
あし	leg, foot
あし の ゆび	toes
あそこ	over there
あそびます	play, muck about
あたたかい	warm
あたま	head
あびます	take (a shower)
あまり	not very, not often
あめ	rain
あらいます	wash
あります	there is (of things)

い

いい ですか	is that OK?
いいます	say
いかが ですか	how about this?
いくら ですか	how much?
いす	chair
いたい	it hurts
いつも	always
いっしょに	together
います	there is (of people, animals)
いや（な）	horrible, terrible
いらっしゃいませ	welcome
いろ	colour

う

うえ	on, above, up
うえき	pot plant
うしろ	behind
うそ	lie
うります	sell
うん	yes, yeah

え

え	picture
エアロビクス	aerobics
エレクトーン	electric organ
えん	yen (currency)

お

おきます	wake up, get up
おげんき ですか	how are you?
おたく	your house
おなか	stomach, tummy
おなか が すいて（い）ます	I'm hungry
おねがい します	may I have?
おふろ	bath
おべんとう	boxed lunch
おみやげ	souvenir
おもしろい	interesting, fun
およぎます	swim
オレンジ ジュース	orange juice

か

か	or
カーテン	curtain
がいこくじん	foreigner
がいじん	foreigner
かえります	return
かお	face
かきます	write, draw
かっこいい	cool, spunky
かぜ	a cold
かみ（のけ）	hair
かめ	turtle
からだ	body

き

き	tree
きいろい	yellow
きせつ	season
ギター	guitar
きます	wear, put on
きょうしつ	classroom
きょねん	last year
きらい（な）	dislike
きれい（な）	pretty, clean
キロ（メートル）	kilo(metres)

く

くち	mouth
くつ	shoes
くま	bear
くもり	cloudy
クラブ	club
クレヨン	crayon
くろい	black

こ

こ、コ	counter for small objects
こうてい	school ground
こうとうがっこう	senior high school
こうこう	senior high school
コーヒー	coffee
ここ	here
こどもたち	children
この ひと	this person, he, she
ゴルフ	golf
こんでいます	crowded

さ

さかな	fish
さくぶん	essay
～さつ	counter for books etc.
ざっし	magazine
さむい	cold

し

ジーンズ	jeans
しけん	examination
じこしょうかい	self-introduction
じしょ	dictionary
しずか（な）	quiet
した	under, below, down
しゃしん	photograph
シャワー	shower
シャンプー	shampoo
しゅうまつ	weekend
じゅぎょう	lesson
しょうかい します	introduce
しょうがっこう	primary school
しょうが ない	can't be helped!
しろい	white
しんじられ ない	that's unbelievable
しんぶん	newspaper

す

すいか	water-melon
すずしい	cool
すてき（な）	nice, lovely
すばらしい	wonderful
スプーン	spoon
すんで います	live

せ

せ	height
せいと	student

せいふく	school uniform
せん	thousand
せんしゅ	player, athlete
ぜんぜん	not at all
ぜんぶ	all, the lot
ぜんぶ で	in all

そ

そこ	there
そして	and then
それから	after that

た

たいいくかん	gymnasium
たいかい	contest
だい	title, topic
だいきらい	hate
たいふう	typhoon
たかい	high, expensive
たくさん	lots, many
たま に	occasionally
だめ	no good
だれ	who?
たんす	wardrobe
ダンス	dance

ち

チャンピオン	champion
ちゅうがっこう	junior high school
ちゅうごく	China
チョコレート	chocolate
ちょっと	a bit

つ

つかいます	use
つくえ	desk
つくります	make
つゆ	rainy season

て

て	hand
でかけます	go out
てがみ	letter
できます	able to do
でしょう	will be
てんき	weather
でんき スタンド	lamp
でんわ	telephone

と

～ど	degrees (temperature)
どうして	why?
ドーナツ	doughnut
どうぶつ	animal
ときどき	sometimes
とけい	watch, clock
とくい	good at
とても、とっても	very
となり	next to
トライアスロン	triathlon
とります	take
トレーニング	training
どんな	what kind of?

な

ナイフ	knife
なか	in
ながい	long
なつ	summer
なにいろ	what colour?
なにご (何語)	what language?
なまけもの	lazy thing
なんにん (何人)	how many people?
なんねんせい	what school level?

に

にく	meat

ね

ねます	go to bed, sleep
～ねんせい	year level student

の

のち	later
のど	throat

は

はいります	enter, come in
はきます	put on, wear
はさみ	scissors
(お)はし	chopsticks
はしります	run
はずかしかった	I'm embarrassed
はな	flower, nose
はなします	speak
はなみ	flower viewing
はやく	quickly, hurry up
はれ	fine weather
パン	bread
ばんごはん	dinner, evening meal
ハンサム (な)	good-looking, handsome

ひ

ピアノ	piano
～ひき	counter for small animals
ひきます	play a stringed instrument, catch (a cold)
ひくい	low
ひと	person
ひどい	dreadful
ひま	free
ひま なとき	spare time
びょういん	hospital
びょうき	sick, ill
ひるやすみ	lunchtime
ピンク (の)	pink

ふ

フォーク	fork
ぶた	pig
ふとりすぎ	too fat
ふります	fall (rain, snow)
ふるい	old (things)
～ふん	minutes
ぶんぼうぐや	stationery shop

へ

ベッド	bed
ペット	pet
ベビー シッター	baby-sitter
へや	room
へん (な)	strange
べんきょう します	study
ベンチ	park bench

ほ

ボールあそび	playing with a ball
ポスト	post box
ホットケーキ	pancake
ホットドッグ	hot dog
～ほん (本)	counter for long, thin objects
ほんばこ	book case

ま

まい...	every...
まいにち	every day
まえ	before, in front of
マスク	(surgical) mask
マジック	highlighter pen
まん	ten thousand

み

みかん	mandarin (orange)
みせ	shop
みじかい	short
みどり (の)	green
みみ	ear

め		
め	eye	
も		
もう	already	
もちろん	of course!	
もの	thing	
や		
〜や	suffix indicating a shop	
やおや	greengrocer	
やさい	vegetable	
やすい	cheap	
やすみ	holiday	
やめて	stop that!	
ゆ		
ゆうめい（な）	famous	
ゆき	snow	
ゆび	finger	
よ		
よい	good	
よく	often	
よく できました	well done	
より	from (in a letter)	
ら		
らいげつ	next month	
り		
りっぱ（な）	great, magnificent	
りんご	apple	
れ		
れいぞうこ	refrigerator	
ろ		
ロックコンサート	rock concert	
わ		
わたし じゃない	not me	
わたしたち	we	

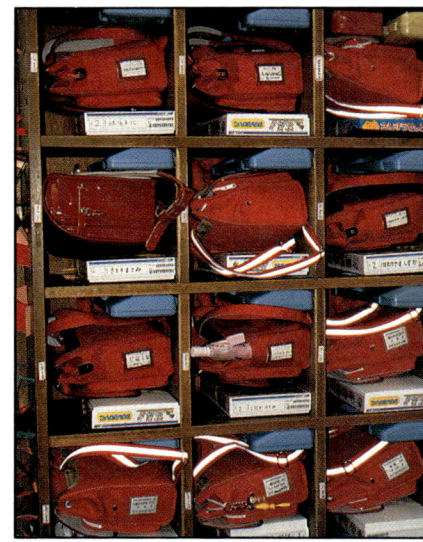
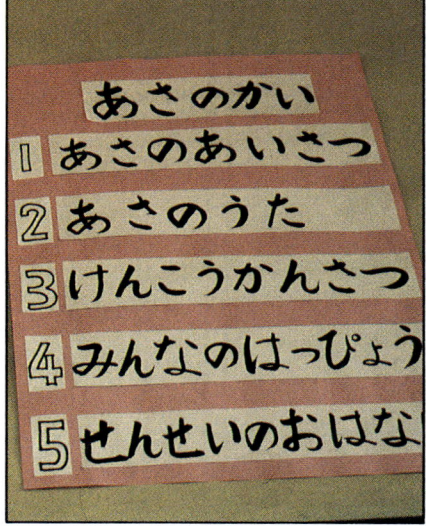
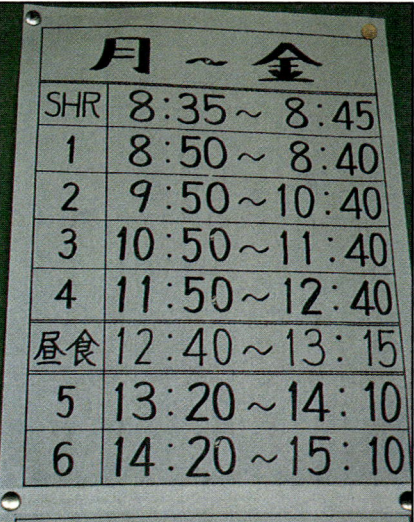

単語・英語―日本語

A
above	うえ
aerobics	エアロビクス
all, the lot	ぜんぶ
already	もう
animal	どうぶつ
apple	りんご
athlete	せんしゅ
autumn	あき

B
bakery	パンや
bath	おふろ
take a bath	おふろに はいります
bear	くま
bed	ベッド
go to bed	ねます
before	まえ
behind	うしろ
below	した
between	あいだ
a bit	ちょっと
black	くろい、ブラック
blue	あおい、ブルー
body	からだ
bookcase	ほんばこ
bread	パン
breakfast	あさごはん

C
chair	いす
cheap	やすい
children	こども、こどもたち
China	ちゅうごく
chopsticks	（お）はし
classroom	きょうしつ
clean	きれい（な）
clock	とけい
cloudy	くもり
cold	さむい
(a) cold	かぜ
have a cold	かぜを ひいて います
colour	いろ
come in, enter	はいります
contest	たいかい
cool	すずしい
cool (spunky)	かっこいい
counters	
for animals	ひき
for books	さつ
for long, thin objects	本
for small objects	こ、つ
crowded	こんで います

D
desk	つくえ
dictionary	じしょ
dinner	ばんごはん
dislike	きらい（な）
down	した
draw	かきます
dreadful	ひどい

E
ear	みみ
electric organ	エレクトーン
enter, come in	はいります
essay	さくぶん
everyday	まいにち
examination	しけん
expensive	たかい
eye	め

F
face	かお
famous	ゆうめい（な）
finger	ゆび
fish	さかな
flower	はな
flower viewing	はなみ
foot	あし
foreigner	がいこくじん、がいじん
free time	ひまなとき
fridge	れいぞうこ
fun	おもしろい

G
get up	おきます
good	よい、いい
go out	でかけます
green	みどり(の)、グリーン
greengrocer	やおや
guitar	ギター
gymnasium	たいいくかん

H
hair	かみ（のけ）
hand	て
handsome	ハンサム（な）
hate	だいきらい
head	あたま
height	せ
high	たかい
holiday	やすみ
horrible	いや（な）
hospital	びょういん
how many people?	なんにん(何人)
how much?	いくら
hungry	おなかが すいて（い）ます
(it) hurts	いたい

I
ice-cream	アイスクリーム
ill	びょうき
in	なか
interesting	おもしろい
introduce	しょうかいします
introduce oneself	じこ しょうかい

J
jeans	ジーンズ

L
leg	あし
letter	てがみ
lie	うそ
live	すんで います
long	ながい
lots	たくさん
low	ひくい
lunch (boxed)	おべんとう
lunchtime	ひるやすみ

M
magazine	ざっし
magnificent	りっぱ（な）
make	つくります
mandarin (orange)	みかん
many	たくさん
meat	にく
morning	あさ
mouth	くち

N
newspaper	しんぶん
next to	となり
nice	すてき（な）

単語 百二十三

nose	はな	scissors	はさみ	wash	あらいます
not much, very	あまり	season	きせつ	watch	とけい
		sell	うります	water-melon	すいか
O		shoes	くつ	we	わたしたち
occasionally	たまに	shop	みせ	wear	
often	よく	short	せがひくい	lower part of body	はきます
old	ふるい	shower	シャワー	top part of body	きます
on	うえ	take a shower	シャワーを あびます	weather	てんき
or	か			cloudy	くもり
over there	あそこ	sick	びょうき	fine	はれ
		snow	ゆき	welcome	いらっしゃいませ
P		it snows	ゆきがふります	what?	なん、なに(何)
person	ひと (人)	sometimes	ときどき	colour?	なにいろ
pet	ペット	sore	いたい	kind of?	どんな
keep pets	ペットを かって います	souvenir	おみやげ	language?	なにご(何語)
		speak	はなします	school year?	なんねんせい
photograph	しゃしん	spunky	かっこいい	white	しろい、ホワイト
picture	え	stationery shop	ぶんぼうぐや	who?	だれ
pig	ぶた	stomach	おなか	why?	どうして
play about	あそびます	strange	へん (な)	wonderful	すばらしい
play a keyboard or stringed instrument	ひきます	student	せいと	write	かきます
		study	べんきょう します		
play a sport	します			**Y**	
player	せんしゅ	summer	なつ	yeah, yes	うん
post box	ポスト	swim	およぎます	year	
pot plant	うえき			last year	きょねん
pretty	きれい (な)	**T**		yellow	きいろい、イエロー
put on		take	とります		
lower part of body	はきます	tall	せがたかい	yen	えん、(円)
top part of body	きます	telephone	でんわ		
		terrible	いや (な)		
Q		there	そこ		
quickly	はやく	thing	もの		
quiet	しずか (な)	thousand	せん		
		throat	のど		
R		title	だい		
rain	あめ	toes	あしのゆび		
it rains	あめがふります	together	いっしょに		
rainy season	つゆ	tree	き		
red	あかい、レッド	turtle	かめ		
refrigerator, fridge	れいぞうこ	typhoon	たいふう		
return	かえります				
room	へや	**U**			
run	はしります	under	した		
		up	うえ		
S		use	つかいます		
say	いいます				
school		**V**			
ground	こうてい	vegetable	やさい		
junior high	ちゅうがっこう	very	とても、とっても		
primary	しょうがっこう				
senior high	こうとうがっこう (こうこう)	**W**			
		wake up	おきます		
uniform	せいふく	wardrobe	たんす		
		warm	あたたかい		